MW00709917

PRAYER & FAITH

TOMMIE J. MATTHEWS

CREATION
HOUSE
A STRANG COMPANY

PRAYER AND FAITH by Tommie Matthews
Published by Creation House
A Strang Company
600 Rinehart Road
Lake Mary, Florida 32746
www.creationhouse.com

This book or parts thereof may not be reproduced in any form, stored in a retrieval system, or transmitted in any form by any means— electronic, mechanical, photocopy, recording, or otherwise—without prior written permission of the publisher, except as provided by United States of America copyright law.

All Scripture quotations are from the King James Version of the Bible.

Hebrew and Greek definitions are derived from *The Dake Annotated Reference Bible* (Lawrenceville, GA: Dake Publishing, 1989).

Author's Note: For the sake of anonymity and confidentiality, the names of certain persons have been changed.

Cover design by Terry Clifton

Copyright © 2005 by Tommie Matthews
All rights reserved

Library of Congress Control Number: 2005930401
International Standard Book Number: 1-59185-878-X

First Edition

05 06 07 08 09 — 987654321
Printed in the United States of America

Dedicated to my grandsons, Marvin II and Benjamin, as they journey on to become men of "prayer and faith."

Acknowledgments

M ANY HAVE CONTRIBUTED to the writing of *Prayer and Faith*. First, I want to thank the Lord for instructing me to write this book, and then bringing to my remembrance my quickly-answered prayers over a period of years.

Thank you to my parents and grandparents, who always encouraged me by telling me that they believed in me.

I am appreciative of educators who, during my early years, demanded nothing less than excellence. Most of them have passed on, but I'm especially grateful to Mrs. Addie P. Owens, who resides in Austin, Texas. She was not only my high school English teacher, but she was also my essay-writing and spelling coach. Mrs. Owens, the hard work paid off.

Kathy Matthews typed the first part of the manuscript while she also read and edited it.

Glenda Hodge typed a portion and entered the entire manuscript into the computer. God bless you, Glenda, for spending all those hours with me.

Bless you, Shelby Lynn, for assisting me.

I am indebted to Doris Couch and Steve Shumaker for allowing the Holy Spirit to use them to confirm the writing of *Prayer and Faith* before I made it known. I will never forget the day Steve called and asked, "How about the book *Prayer and Faith*?" Wow!

Last, but not least, I want to thank the members of Morning Star Church and my pastor, W. A. Sesley. They have prayed for me and asked about the book.

Mother Mosetta Miller, you did what I requested of you. You motivated me by asking, "How is the book coming?" Thank you much.

Contents

Foreword

"I⠀T'S ALREADY DONE." These three little words—a message our mother delivered—changed our lives forever and took our faith to a new level. It became very obvious to us that God has already done what we ask if we believe it and if it is in His will. We now know for ourselves that faith without belief is dead.

As long as we can remember, our mother told us that our great-grandmother, Nanny, laid the foundation for her faith walk. Since my grandmother raised my mother, she too has unbelievable faith.

As children, we did not appreciate our mother's relationship with God, nor could we comprehend her prayer life and her great faith. You see, Mother's prayer life was incredible. Even though we did not understand her devout prayer life, we did notice that whatever she prayed, God did it!

Realizing the importance of prayer, our mother encouraged Marvin and me to pray fervently. She made us aware of the power of prayer and told us to pray, believing that God was moving on our behalf. We were also taught that God allows certain trials in our lives to strengthen us—*without tests, there are no testimonies.*

We thank God for our praying mother. As a family, we have witnessed God's remarkable results through prayer. Moreover, we can attest to the miracles that God has performed for our mother, family members, many, many others, and us.

In closing, what once was a mystery to us is now a reality. We now pray, believing that God has already done what we have requested. What a blessing to know that God is waiting on us to receive what He desires for us! Mom, thank you for teaching us that prayer changes things.

Again, thanks Mama!

—Nataline Matthews Woods
Marvin Matthews

Chapter 1

My Grandmother—A Woman of Prayer and Faith

L ET ME TELL you about *m-y-y-y* grandmother.
It seems that most African American success stories evolve because of the presence and involvement of grandmothers. The term of endearment may be "Nana," "Nanny," "Big Mama," "Little Mama," "Mother Dear," "Muh Dear," "Mother," "Granma," "Grandmother," or "Momma." But they are our parents' mothers, and they are so special.

Many athletes, preachers, politicians, and others honor their grandmothers for steering them in the right direction. One noted gospel singer testifies in song, "I had a praying grandmother."

Perhaps grandmother stories are not common only to African American families. In 2 Timothy 1, Paul writes of Timothy's faith and heritage:

> I thank God, whom I serve from my forefathers with pure conscience, that without ceasing I have remembrance of thee in my prayers night and day; greatly desiring to see thee, being mindful of thy tears, that I may be filled with joy; when I call to remembrance the unfeigned faith that is in thee, which dwelt first in thy grandmother Lois, and thy mother Eunice; and I am persuaded that in thee also.
> —2 TIMOTHY 1:3–5

Lois apparently communicated her faith to Eunice, and no doubt both Lois and Eunice communicated their faith to

1

Timothy. A Christian upbringing and a spiritual family atmosphere are decided advantages.

My grandmother—Nanny, as I affectionately called her—was a rare breed. She was definitely unlike anyone else I have known. Nanny was strong, fearless, proud, and outspoken (too much so). She was not a hypocrite. If she did not particularly care for an individual, the person knew it. She was ever so honest, and I learned to read her well.

Whenever I questioned the veracity of another family member's statement, I would go and ask her if it was true. If it was, she would say, "Yes, that's right." If it was not, she would say, "Well, that's what he said." From her response, I knew the answer to my question. She would not be in cahoots with a liar.

Nanny—also known as Mrs. Whitfield—was a disciplinarian. She delighted in administering a good old-fashioned whipping. The victim would then have to show the welts to other relatives as she boasted, "I tore him/her up." I can truthfully say she was no respecter of persons. Unlike family relationships today, her grandchildren were not exempt. They were disciplined the same way her children were.

On one occasion, one of her children's friends was in the wrong place at the wrong time. It was one of those situations we all found ourselves in when we broke curfew and were afraid to go into the house. Of course, the next best thing was to go in with a buffer—a person or friend who was with you. This act was designed to at least postpone the beating. According to the story, this plan did not work. Her son got the belt, and his friend got it, too.

Nanny put the counsel of Proverbs 23 into action:

> Withhold not correction from the child: for if thou beatest him with the rod, he shall not die. Thou shalt beat him with the rod, and shalt deliver his soul from hell.
> —Proverbs 23:13–14

We are not privileged to know who the writer of Hebrews was, but he evidently knew the likes of Nanny because he mentioned fathers who "verily for a few days chastened us after their own pleasure" (Heb. 12:10). Speaking of the fathers in verse 9, he said, "…and we gave them reverence." I give Nanny reverence in this section.

Nanny was very supportive of her children and grandchildren. We were involved in both church and school activities. There were programs accompanied by many rehearsals, athletic competitions with hours of practice, and literary events that required weeks of preparation. Mrs. Whitfield encouraged us to work hard in all these undertakings, and she actually attended some of the athletic contests in which we participated.

When I was in eighth grade, my school sponsored a queen contest. Of course, it was a fundraiser, and the girl who raised the most money would represent the school as homecoming queen. At first, only the girls in grades nine to twelve were eligible to participate. For some reason, however, the rule was changed to include eighth graders, and I was drafted to represent my class. Mrs. Thelma Teal, an English teacher from Waco, Texas, was my sponsor.

My entire family—especially my grandmother—supported me. We sold beautiful aprons that she made, and I won out over the senior class representative by a total of only twenty-five dollars. I don't remember, but I would like to think that we sold twenty-five-dollar's worth of aprons. I was crowned Miss Homecoming of Wilson White High School, Rosebud, Texas, at the age of twelve.

My grandmother was an extremely hard worker who did housework for people who lived on the other side of town. The railroad tracks were the demarcation line for the blacks and whites of our town. Nanny cooked for diner owners, did day work, and picked and chopped cotton.

It was amazing how far she stretched a dollar. The lady single-handedly paid for my college education. She did not depend on anyone else's contribution. If any other person promised to help with room and board, she would say, "Listen, if he sends it, hold it until next month. I won't depend on it." She made sure every penny was there on time.

Praise God for my grandmother who was strong, fearless, proud, outspoken, honest, disciplinarian, and supportive. But in retrospect, her strong belief in the power of prayer and her faith in God impacted my life the most. She lived the following words of Jesus:

> For verily I say unto you, that whosoever shall say unto
> this mountain, be thou removed, and be thou cast into
> the sea; and shall not doubt in his heart, but shall believe
> that those things which he saith shall come to pass; he
> shall have whatsoever he saith. Therefore I say unto you,
> what things soever ye desire, when ye pray, believe that
> ye receive them, and ye shall have them.
>
> —MARK 11:23–24

Prayer was a way of life in our household. It preceded and accompanied every major decision.

Nanny made intercession for her family as well as for herself. She believed God for deliverance of all kinds: healing, jobs, promotions, college opportunities, and whatever she desired. She was definitely one who did not limit God. As a result, God moved miraculously in our midst.

Very often she solicited prayer help from the pastor—the man of God. In a sense, he was her prayer partner. I was the one who was selected to carry the written note, a prayer request accompanied by an offering, to the pastor's house. If the pastor lived in another city, she was not hindered by distance; she mailed the request to him.

Isn't it something how she blessed the man of God because he stood in the gap for her family?

> Let him that is taught in the word communicate unto
> him that teacheth in all good things.
>
> —GALATIANS 6:6

She greatly appreciated the labor of ministers, and she esteemed them very highly in love for their work's sake.

> And we beseech you, brethren, to know them which
> labour among you, and are over you in the Lord, and
> admonish you; and to esteem [Greek word *perissos*
> means "beyond measure"] them very highly in love for
> their work's sake.
>
> —1 THESSALONIANS 5:12–13

I have no doubt that God predestined my grandmother to raise me because of His call upon my life. At the time, neither she nor

I knew that an impartation was taking place. Webster defines the word *impartation* as giving or granting what one has by contact, association, or influence; to communicate or transmit.

Consider how God has already used that which was given to me through my association with my grandmother.

Impartation took place in the following areas:

1. Respect your minister.

In 1982, I was appointed number one assistant to my pastor. At the time of this writing, I still hold this position. It was controversial to some, for I am the first female to work in this area. It is of no controversy to me because God placed me there. In the words of Romans 8:31, "If God be for [you], who can be against [you]?"

> He that receiveth you receiveth me, and he that receiveth me receiveth him that sent me.
> —MATTHEW 10:40

Just as Nanny did in her lifetime, I esteem my pastor very highly in love for his work's sake. Not only does my leader receive my respect, but any man or woman of God who graces the podium has my respect. If this person is in error, he or she is God's errant preacher.

> Who art thou that judgest another man's servant? to his own master he standeth or falleth. Yea, he shall be holden up: for God is able to make him stand.
> —ROMAN 14:4

God has the responsibility to deal with His servant. And I have the responsibility to pray for him. I knew Nanny forty-two years, and not one time did I hear her speak ill of a preacher. Praise God! What a testimony!

2. Prayer and faith.

God has made great use of that which Nanny communicated or transmitted to me in the area of prayer and faith. How else would I be able to share these testimonies with the body of Christ and other readers?

Like other believers, I sometimes struggle in the area of trusting God. But it helps to be able to recall what God did for us as a family during my youth. Praise Him!

I was taught that God can do anything—absolutely anything that we can believe He will do. Genesis 18:14 asks the rhetorical question, "Is any thing too hard for the Lord?" Matthew 19:26 adds, "But Jesus beheld them, and said unto them, With men this is impossible; but with God all things are possible."

The glorious truth of the matter is this: that which was imparted to me—especially teaching in the area of prayer and faith—has been passed on to my children. The Word of the Lord is explicit regarding the duties of parents and to children:

> And these words, which I command thee this day, shall be in thine heart: and thou shalt teach them diligently unto thy children, and shalt talk of them when thou sittest in thine house, and when thou walkest by the way, and when thou liest down, and when thou risest up. And thou shalt bind them for a sign upon thine hand, and they shall be as frontlets between thine eyes. And thou shalt write them upon the posts of thy house, and on thy gates.
>
> —Deuteronomy 6:6–9

On the other hand, children are instructed to listen to their parents.

The following Scripture verses give four commandments to children, and six blessings for those who are obedient to their fathers and mothers, as prescribed by the Word of God:

> My son, keep thy father's commandment, and forsake not the law of thy mother: bind them continually upon thine heart, and tie them about thy neck. When thou goest, it shall lead thee; when thou sleepest, it shall keep thee; and when thou awakest, it shall talk with thee. For the commandment is a lamp; and the law is light; and reproofs of instruction are the way of life.
>
> —Proverbs 6:20–23

Praise God for His Word. As Psalm 119:105 says, it is indeed "a lamp unto my feet, and a light unto my path."

3. Intercession.

The prayer ministry of the church has always been of great interest to me. I am well acquainted with the necessity of, and the blessing a person receives from, spending time in his prayer closet. The communion that I experience in my private chamber is divine bliss.

> But thou, when thou prayest, enter into thy closet, and when thou hast shut thy door, pray to thy Father which is in secret; and thy Father which seeth in secret shall reward thee openly.
>
> —MATTHEW 6:6

But there is power in united prayer. Besides the general regard God has to the prayers of the saints, He is particularly pleased with their union and communion.

> Behold, how good and how pleasant it is for brethren to dwell together in unity!
>
> —PSALM 133:1

> Again I say unto you, That if two of you shall agree on earth as touching any thing that they shall ask, it shall be done for them of my Father which is in heaven. For where two or three are gathered together in my name, there am I in the midst of them.
>
> —MATTHEW 18:19–20

> And when they had prayed, the place was shaken where they were assembled together; and they were all filled with the Holy Ghost, and they spake the word of God with boldness.
>
> —ACTS 4:31

After I retired from my secular job, the Lord placed it upon my heart to call together church members who would commit to praying for every aspect of the ministry, from the pulpit to the nursery. The response was great, and many of these individuals now make up the church's intercessory team, which prays without ceasing.

When we first embarked upon the ministry of intercession, there was much we did not know. We are enrolled into the "University of Intercession," and the Holy Spirit is our Instructor, Dean, and President. He has taught us well, and He continues to work in us, through us, and for us in the area of intercessory prayer.

Ongoing interest in the area of prayer has grown from the seed of intercession that was sown in my spirit years ago. It was just waiting to spring forth, and in God's appointed time, it did.

As I reflect upon my relationship with my grandmother, I have unanswered questions. However, I am sure that God's sovereign purpose was accomplished and is being accomplished as a result of my upbringing in Nanny's house.

God is sovereign. He can do what He wants to when He wants.

I thank God for being God, and I thank Him for *my-y-y-y-y* grandmother.

Chapter 2

Lord, I Want
the Holy Spirit Tonight

As I neared the point of total surrender to the Lord, I began to think about being filled with the Holy Spirit with the evidence of speaking in tongues. I wondered what it would be like, and the more I thought about this, the more excited I became about the idea of receiving Him. I really believe that it was the expectation of the baptism in the Holy Spirit that caused me to finally say, "Yes, Lord, here I am. I totally surrender to you."

I can relate to the lyrics of the song "Just As I Am":

Just as I am, without one plea,
But that Thy blood was shed for me,
And that Thou bid'st me come to Thee,
O Lamb of God, I come! I come!

Just as I am, tho' tossed about,
With many a conflict, many a doubt,
Fightings and fears within, without,
O Lamb of God, I come! I come!

It was time for me to say, "Here I am, Lord; I surrender to you just as I am." I was a faithful churchgoer, church worker, and Sunday school teacher; a financially supporting Christian. Yet, I had run from the Lord for years, and I was tired, tired, tired. I do not have one of those drug-addiction, prostitution, alcoholic, did-everything testimonies, but I needed Jesus in a great way.

The church had always been a part of my life. My mother

bought me my first Bible (or "Bable," as I called it) when I was four years old. In all the years from age four until thirty-six, I never confessed Jesus as Lord and Savior. But on October 13, 1974, I accepted God's greatest gift—His Son, who died for my offenses and was raised from the dead for my justification. If just thinking about the Holy Spirit caused such a stirring in me before salvation, one can only imagine the joy that flooded my soul after I was saved.

Now that I had been born of the Spirit and belonged to Jesus, I knew that the baptism in the Holy Spirit was mine for the asking. Luke 11:13 says that if we ask for the Holy Spirit, our prayer will be answered.

During the midweek service two weeks after I had received the Lord Jesus, my pastor asked us to come to the altar for prayer. Standing there, I said from the depths of my heart, *Lord, I want the Holy Spirit tonight.* It was an inner prayer. I did not speak it with my lips, but God heard it, and that was most important. After leading us in prayer, the pastor announced, "You may take your seats." By the time I reached my seat, I was speaking in tongues, as the Spirit gave me utterance:

> And they were all filled with the Holy Ghost, and began to speak with other tongues, as the Spirit gave them utterance.
>
> —ACTS 2:4

Praise God! He answered that prayer immediately.

Chapter 3

Single Parent

HAVING BEEN THRUST into the role of a single parent, it did not take me long to realize that the term *single parent* is a misnomer. It should be *double parent*—one person acting as two parents. What an impossibility! I had to ask myself how to handle this. *What is of utmost importance in my life?*

The answer was my God, my children, and my job. I resolved to remain faithful to my God, who is my Source. I kept attending church services regularly and continued in my positions of youth director and Sunday school teacher. Besides holding a highly analytical job where I supervised others, I had two teen-aged children. I tried hard to nurture them wholly—mentally, emotionally, and spiritually.

I quickly learned that life goes on. The world does not stop to let you off. You either hang on, or you fall off. Praise God, I hung on and weathered the storm!

> If thou faint in the day of adversity, thy strength is small.
> —PROVERBS 24:10

The saints prayed, the Lord strengthened us, and we kept moving. We moved slowly at first, but we did not lie down and die.

In addition to my job and my children, I was faced with the upkeep of my home and my automobile. Periodically, things broke down and repairs were needed. I had to rely upon the Lord. If I had not, I would have lost my mind.

My mind? Oh no! I had to keep a sound mind, for He gave it to me.

> For God hath not given us the spirit of fear; but of power, and of love, and of a sound mind.
>
> —2 TIMOTHY 1:7

> And be not conformed [Greek word *suschematizo* means "to conform to another's example"] to this world: but be ye transformed [Greek word *metamorphor* means "transformed or transfigured by a supernatural change"] by the renewing of your mind, that ye may prove what is that good, and acceptable, and perfect, will of God.
>
> —ROMANS 12:2

My mind? Oh no! I had to be renewed in the spirit of my mind.

> And be renewed in the spirit of your mind.
>
> —EPHESIANS 4:23

My mind? Oh no! I had to take on the mind of Christ.

> Let this mind be in you, which was also in Christ Jesus.
>
> —PHILIPPIANS 2:5

As I stated before, home repairs were sometimes needed. On one particular occasion, a leak in the den ceiling had caused water damage. The stain grew larger and uglier, and I knew that I needed a dependable painter who was capable of redoing the entire ceiling. This sounds easy enough, but the first lesson I learned as a single parent is that people do not always keep their word. Many have no problem *under*doing but *over*charging. I needed a word from the Lord, and I sought His counsel. It was a simple prayer of five words, "Lord, I need a painter."

Several days passed, and my doorbell rang. There at my door stood a tall gentleman who gave the answer to my prayer in five words, "Ma'am, I am a painter." Needless to say, I hired the man on the spot. He did an outstanding job for the price of fifty dollars.

> For the eyes of the Lord are over the righteous, and his ears are open unto their prayers.
>
> —1 PETER 3:12

Praise God! He did it again.

Chapter 4

Marvin

⁓‿◦

M Y SON, MARVIN, aspired to become a civil engineer. After graduating from high school, he entered Christian Brothers University in Memphis, Tennessee. At the time, the engineering department at Christian Brothers ranked ninth in the United States.

Upon completion of his freshman year, he said that he felt a call from God to preach the gospel of Jesus Christ. This did not come as a surprise. He had carried his Bible to school during his high school years, and people had referred to him as "the boy with the Bible." In response to God's call, he left Christian Brothers University and enrolled at East Texas Bible College in Tyler, Texas.

It was there that he met Carol Frison from Millens, Georgia. Carol was already preaching the gospel of Jesus Christ, and had worked tent revivals with her pastor in Georgia. But Carol also felt the leading of the Lord to go to east Texas to increase her knowledge of the Word of God. Anyway, Marvin and Carol became good friends and were married two years later. They continued to reside in Texas after their wedding and eventually purchased a home there.

Marvin had several good jobs in Texas, and they fared well as beginners. But his heart's desire was to complete the required college courses for his engineering degree and secure work in that area.

My daughter recently reminded me that I very often spoke these words, "Marvin will get his engineering degree." The Lord told me in his Word:

What things soever [I] desire, when [I] pray, believe that [I] receive them, and [I] shall have them.

—MARK 11:24

And whatsoever [I] shall ask in [His] name, that will [He] do, that the Father may be glorified in the Son.

—JOHN 14:13

He said it, I believed it, and I only began to say what He said. In essence, He said that if I asked in faith in His name, I would receive it.

This is why I could say without trepidation, "Marvin will get his engineering degree." Bless God for His Word!

I knew all along that it would take God to work it out. Marvin had a slight problem because he had started his engineering course work in Memphis, Tennessee, and he was now living in Tyler, Texas. As I looked at the situation, I saw impossibility. However, as Luke 1:37 says, "With God nothing shall be impossible."

After much discourse with our pastor, a breakthrough came in 1988. Marvin decided to move his family to Memphis, where he was employed by the church as business administrator. Although Marvin seemed to enjoy this work, his first love was videography. This had been evident when he brought his camcorder along on visits from Texas to Memphis and taped our worship services. He did an absolutely marvelous job in this area.

A short while after Marvin's move to Memphis, the church purchased its own television broadcast system, including cameras and editing equipment. Marvin moved from administration to videography and absorbed himself in intense study of every aspect of the setup. Before long, he and a team of young men were not only taping and editing our services for television broadcast, but their services were sought after and made available to other churches and businesses.

The chief advantage for Marvin was that he could work day and night or sometimes all night if he needed to meet a deadline. In fact, when he edited, he chose to work alone at night in order to avoid interruptions.

After he had been back in Memphis for five years, he decided to check with the appropriate officials at the university to see how many credit hours he needed for graduation. *Praise Him! Praise Him! Praise Him!*

Marvin's advisor did not paint a rosy picture, but Marvin charted his course-work path with the intention to graduate. Yes, a wife, two sons, a job, and fifteen years later he enrolled again. This time he pursued a degree in electrical engineering.

At noon, May 11, 1996, Marvin received his degree.

I had said, "Marvin will get his degree."

If ye shall ask any thing in my name, I will do it.

—JOHN 14:14

Chapter 5

Valley State

⌒

THE MEMPHIS CITY School System implemented the string program as part of its music curriculum when my daughter, Nataline, was in fourth grade. She and several of her classmates entered the program. Of course, this meant that we, the parents, had to purchase violins. I did not mind, for I was highly impressed that such a prestigious program was made available for our children.

Pleasantly, she endured. Nataline and one of her male classmates in the graduating class of 1977 were the only two members who had remained in the string program since they joined it in the fourth grade.

In the fall of 1977, she entered Spelman College. We managed financially her freshman year, but I knew that her second year would be a bit more difficult. In addition, at the end of her first year, she wanted to transfer from Spelman. Along with several other friends, she hoped to go to the University of Tennessee at Knoxville. A transfer, particularly to UT at Knoxville, did not set well with me. Finally, I said, "Okay, one transfer; that's it." But I was not settled as to where she should go if she left Spelman.

One day, as I was working at the laboratory, a young lady who served as a clerk called for me to come up front. "Tommie," she told me, "Mississippi Valley State University (MVSU) is looking for and recruiting anyone who plays a violin. In fact, they are giving scholarships to those students."

I immediately knew that the Lord had heard my prayer for money for the rest of Nataline's education. I knew that this was of God. I also realized why she had continued as a member of

17

the string program all those years. She had not really been overwhelmed at the prospect of being a violinist.

God had ordained the scholarship for Nataline before the foundation of the world. Second Peter 1:3 says, "According as his divine power hath given unto us all things that pertain unto life and godliness, through the knowledge of him that hath called us to glory and virtue."

When I told her about the scholarship, she was not thrilled about a transfer to MVSU; but I was quite satisfied. We paid a visit to the campus and were pleasantly surprised at the modern buildings and facilities. Nataline applied to the school and was soon accepted in the program. She was awarded a music scholarship for violin and adjusted to her new environment, as I knew she would. My daughter spent three wonderful years there.

From a financial point of view, this situation worked well on several levels. First, the violin scholarship covered the major expenses such as tuition, fees, and housing—all items we had paid for ourselves when she was enrolled at Spelman. In addition, we also had the transportation costs of airline tickets when she was at Spelman. However, since Mississippi Valley was less than one hundred miles from Memphis, we could save money by simply picking her up when she needed to come home. At times, she could ride home with someone who was traveling to our area.

From a religious point of view, a great move of God was happening among Pentecostal believers on campus. They held a weekly service in the gymnasium, and Nataline met many men and women of like faith.

Educationally, the Lord prepared her well in the field of English, and she graduated on schedule with a good grade point average.

Now when I tease Nataline about her initial response to Valley State, as it is called, she says, "It's OK. That's where I met Jeannie." Jeannie remains one of her closest friends. As a matter of fact, she was Jeannie's maid of honor, and Jeannie was one of her matrons of honor.

We give God honor, glory, and praise because He opened the door so that Nataline could walk right through it. And she did it with His divine help.

Chapter 6

Condo

⌒

NATALINE AND HER friends Ada and Mattie went "eye buying" for houses on a beautiful Sunday afternoon. Nataline fell in love with an appealing condominium that was valued at $84,000, a price she could not nearly afford. Besides, the Lord had already blessed her with a two-bedroom house, complete with one bathroom, a living room with a fireplace, a small sitting room, a huge kitchen, and a large backyard. It was ideal for a young, single woman.

Several months later, Ada's friend, who owned a condominium, got married. She needed a buyer for her place so she and her husband would be free to purchase a new home together. Ada immediately remembered that Nataline had expressed a desire to own a condominium and told her newlywed friend that she knew someone who might purchase her condo.

Ada arranged a meeting between the two young ladies and introduced them, and the talks began. An agreement was reached whereby Nataline would make a down payment of $1,000 prorated over a period of one year, and assume the existing loan. Of course, it was not difficult to find a renter for Nataline's neat little house.

After she closed on the property and her house was rented to a matronly woman who appeared to be responsible, Nataline moved from Atlanta, Georgia, to within five miles of her job. Before this, she had commuted fifty miles round-trip from Atlanta to the school where she worked. The new situation was such an advantage! Things appeared to be going well for her.

Then the telephone call came. Yes, a telephone call came from

Nataline's attorney, who had some startling information. The bank had notified him that only a first-time homeowner was eligible to assume the loan on the condo. Since Nataline had already purchased a home, she was ineligible. As a matter of fact, the clause not only prohibited her from buying the condo, it also denied her the right to rent the property.

What a predicament! Her house was rented, and she was broke because she had spent her savings on the move. She was in desperate need of an attorney, and the fee would be no less than $750. All I could say was, "Lord, fix it for my child."

I had no doubt that He was going to work it out. When I talked to her, I would feed her these words, "I don't know what God is going to do, but He's going to fix it." Poor girl. She was distraught, to say the least.

We talked, we prayed, and I held to the fact that God was going to fix it. The apostle Paul said:

> Now unto him that is able to do exceeding abundantly above all that we ask or think, according to the power that worketh in us.
>
> —Ephesians 3:20

After a while, I saw faith come alive within Nataline. She started looking for another condo and found one she loved. It had five levels, much like the one she had seen on that first eye-buying house hunt. It was valued at around $80,000.

Nataline remained in a chaotic situation. She did not have even one hundred dollars in her bank account. In church, we use the phrase that "her back was up against the wall." Was it ever! But God makes the difference in our circumstances. He allows us the setup so that we may be blessed.

One day, Nataline was outside, and Pat, a neighbor, stopped to say hello. Nataline's response was "Hi, I'm homeless. I don't have a home."

Of course, Pat wanted to know what she meant. My daughter explained, and it turned out that this neighbor was there by divine appointment. She told Nataline that real estate agents can trade homes for some buyers. "If the real estate personnel can find someone to assume your loan," she said, "the down payment will become yours to pay on another piece of property."

Nataline contacted the proper authority, who found an interested buyer for the questionable condo. However, she still needed a lawyer, and she surely did not have $750. Finally, one of her attorney friends offered his help. He said, "I'm not a real-estate lawyer, but I'll do all I can to help you. I will not charge you a fee."

Praise God!

All concerned parties—the original owner and her attorney; the new buyer and her attorney; and Nataline—came together. Nataline's attorney friend could not attend the session, but he represented her via telephone. Maybe the Lord planned it so that an attorney in the flesh would not be present on her behalf. God was Nataline's representative, and did He ever work it out!

The new buyer, in addition to assuming the loan, made a down payment of $4,000. This was passed on to Nataline to be used as a down payment on the new condo. Also, she was reimbursed the $1,000 down payment on the original condo purchase, and compensated for her moving expenses as well.

What an attorney! Attorney Jesus!

By the way, the new condominium is located approximately one mile from Nataline's job. Not twenty-five miles, not five miles, but *one* mile.

The first condo was valued at only $60,000. The second one was valued at $80,000, but after negotiations, she was able to purchase it for $73,000.

> But as for you, ye thought evil against me; but God meant it unto good.
>
> —Genesis 50:20

Chapter 7

My Mother

MY MOTHER IS the eldest of five children. (Because her mother raised me, I was considered the sixth child.) She is a lovely lady who loves life and acknowledges it with a hearty laugh. She was raised in the church, but like so many others, she strayed away when she reached a certain age.

As a matter of fact, from my childhood days until 1993, she was not a regular churchgoer. I was very troubled by this, and I prayed without ceasing, *Lord, save my mother.* I was troubled not only because she was not saved, but also because, in 1993, she was an aged woman who did not know the Lord.

Statistics show that most people come to the Lord before the age of fifty. In other words, if an individual is not saved by the time he is fifty years old, he may never come to know Jesus as Lord and Savior. I was not aware of this in 1993, and had I known it, I believe I would have prayed even harder.

You see, I firmly believe that "the effectual fervent prayer of a righteous man availeth much" (James 5:16). Also, I am of the mind-set that there are some things the Lord has to do for me. He has to save all my loved ones, and that settles that.

Second Peter 3:9 says that the Lord "is longsuffering to us-ward, not willing that any should perish, but that all should come to repentance." Since this is true, someone should be standing in the gap for the lost.

And I sought for a man among them, that should make up
the hedge, and stand in the gap before me for the land, that
I should not destroy it: but I found none. Therefore have I
poured out mine indignation upon them; I have consumed
them with the fire of my wrath: their own way have I rec-
ompensed upon their heads, saith the Lord GOD.

—EZEKIEL 22:30–31

I could think of no greater one for whom I should make up
the hedge and stand in the gap than my mother, the one who
brought me into this world. Yes, I cried out to the Lord on her
behalf day and night, and He heard my cry. I have heard it said
that the Lord works in mysterious ways, His wonders to perform.
He does.

In 1989, my mother discovered a lump in her right breast. She
immediately went to her family doctor, who referred her to a surgeon in another town. The surgeon did a biopsy, which showed
cancer in her right breast. Since the cancer had not spread, only a
partial mastectomy was necessary. We were all somewhat shaken,
but I saw the hand of God at work in her life.

I have come to realize that when God begins to move in a
situation as a result of my prayers, I have to cry sometimes. But
I have learned to close my eyes, grit my teeth, turn my head, and
let Him work.

It was when my mother realized the presence of cancer in her
body that she totally surrendered her life to the Lord.

In everything give thanks for this is the will of God in
Christ Jesus concerning you.

—1 THESSALONIANS 5:18

Chapter 8

Daddy

M Y MOTHER MARRIED my stepfather when I was four-years-old. As a matter of fact, I was one of the two other people (besides the preacher) who were present at the wedding. Daddy (I've always called him "Daddy") is a wonderful husband and father.

As a husband, he has always been attentive to my mother. As far back as I can remember, they have always taken evening drives, just the two of them. Very often, the extent of their drive was to go up and down Main Street several times and come back home. Now they venture to one or more neighboring towns, as far as twenty-five miles away. When it is warm, they sit outside on the porch at night until the early morning hours. This is indicative of the lifestyle of small town dwellers.

As a younger man, he coached Little League baseball teams. The teams consisted of any boy who desired to play. Race did not matter. He did a great job with these children, not only as coach but also as a teacher. Daddy took time to teach them about life. He taught self-respect as well as respect for others. In spite of these fine qualities, he, like all human beings, had a serious flaw. Daddy had a drinking problem. In fact, he was an alcoholic until 1971.

I thank God for my mother's loyalty and persistence. She talks about the quality of persistence that I possess, and I am an unusually persistent person. However, I suspect that I inherited that trait from her. She did not give up; she simply refused to leave Daddy or divorce him. I am not saying that she was happy with the situation, but she had faith that a change would take place.

Bless her. She employed the tactics that had worked so well

for her mother—Nanny, my grandmother, the woman of prayer and faith. Mother began to solicit prayer for Daddy's deliverance from alcohol. They did not have a pastor because at that time, and they did not even attend church on a regular basis. However, we all loved and respected my aunt's pastor, who prayed for Daddy. Praise God! The Lord delivered him from the bondage of alcoholism. His was not an instant deliverance, but he began to drink less and less. After a while, he stopped drinking altogether. God did it.

Daddy did join a small Methodist church, which met a few times a month. However, he needed more than church membership. He needed Jesus. After my mother was saved in 1993, I had a prayer partner as I prayed for Daddy. As I said, "Lord, save Daddy," she was saying, "Lord, save my husband."

He started attending some church services with Mother and he thoroughly enjoyed them. In 1994, at the age of 76, Daddy accepted the Lord. How wonderful! I still praise the Lord for these two souls who were saved in their later years. After both of them were saved, this was my prayer: *Lord, now that they both are saved, give them time here on earth to work together for you. Lord, they have always loved each other and have done things together. Now, since they both love you, let them do a work for you.*

It is not unusual for me to call them and find them making preparations for a church dinner or program. On one occasion, I asked Daddy, "What have you been doing today?" He responded, "Well, I cut the church yard today." Just a short while ago, my mother informed me that she had been working at the church and that she was going back to turn on the air conditioner for the evening service.

They have great opportunities to work in their church because the pastor and his family live approximately twenty-five miles from the church. My parents have a key to the small building and can do whatever is necessary.

They are energized by what they do for the Lord and for the church. It is a blessing to hear them talk about their services and their church family. They dearly love their pastor and his family. I dearly love them, and I am still in awe of God and His work in their lives.

I want to encourage each one who reads this testimony to hold fast in prayer for your loved ones. Don't ever give up! We must snatch them from Satan's grasp.

> Our soul is escaped as a bird out of the snare of the fowlers: the snare is broken, and we are escaped. Our help is in the name of the LORD, who made heaven and earth.
>
> —PSALM 124:7–8

We can only accomplish this through the power of prayer. No amount of rebuke, chastisement, works of wisdom, coercion, appealing to their right senses, or any other tactic will work. Only prayer will cause the conviction of the Holy Spirit to engulf an individual.

> As it is written, There is none righteous, no, not one: There is none that understandeth, there is none that seeketh after God. They are all gone out of the way, they are together become unprofitable; there is none that doeth good, no, not one.
>
> —ROMANS 3:10–12

> No man can come to me, except the Father which hath sent me draw him: and I will raise him up at the last day.
>
> —JOHN 6:44

Chapter 9

Daddy Hamilton

M Y DADDY, WHO resided in Oklahoma City, Oklahoma, died in May 1979. My aunt called with the news that he had been found dead in bed and said that I needed to come as soon as possible to make the funeral arrangements. Within a day or so, I was off to Oklahoma City. I really did not have a choice in the matter.

Daddy had been divorced for several years, and I was the older of two children. He also had a teenaged son who was born during my sophomore year in college. Strangely enough, I had never seen John. I feel that this was because Daddy and I did not communicate. Also, John's mother moved them to another city after the divorce, and I had no idea where they lived. So the responsibility of making funeral plans was all mine.

I could not believe that daddy was dead at the age of fifty-nine. *That's too young to die*, I thought. Naturally, my thoughts soon turned to where he would spend eternity. I did not know.

I had last seen Daddy in August 1974, two months before I became a Christian. I was in Oklahoma City for a first cousin's funeral, and he and a friend had come to my aunt's house to see me. It did not enter my mind that this would be the last time I would see him alive.

My testimony is not unlike that of others who confess the name of Christ. As soon as we are saved, we earnestly desire the salvation of family members. Not only did I not see my daddy from 1974 to 1979, but I also did not correspond with him in any way. Yet, I surely prayed for him. I simply said, "Lord, save my daddy." My heart had a burning desire that my daddy would come to know the Lord. I would say it again, "Lord, save my daddy."

So now I had to plan his funeral. I did not know if he attended church or not. I had no way of knowing if anyone had given him a gospel tract or verbally had given him the plan of salvation. The Lord knew what was on my heart. He knew all the questions that troubled me. He is so mindful of us, and He wants us to be at peace.

After I arrived in Oklahoma City and settled in at my aunt and uncle's house, they began to tell me about Daddy's last days. My aunt said that Daddy had been undecided about where he wanted to spend his vacation. He had been torn between going to Memphis or Texas. She had preferred that he go to Memphis rather than Texas. Considering the fact that he no longer drank, he would have been encouraged to drink with old friends in Texas. When she said this to him, Daddy's reply was, "Aunt Sara, I don't want anything to drink. Someone is praying for me."

Praise Him! Praise Him! Praise Him! Praise Him!

She was not finished. I sat there stunned as she continued. She related that he had acquired an interest in himself. He had purchased new clothes and had his car painted. Most importantly, although he had lived with a woman, he had moved out. Aunt Sara did not realize that the Holy Spirit was prompting her to share this with me.

Let me give God all His glory by sharing what friends in Texas said about Daddy. My uncle said he was so different that he thought something was wrong with him.

I wanted to run, jump, scream, shout, and holler—all at the same time! I soon found out that I should have done all of the above. Little did I know that I needed a good praise.

Aunt Sara and Uncle Bob had chosen Rosebud Funeral Home to pick up the body. I had no idea where burial money would come from because I did not know anything about Daddy's business affairs. Immediately I went to Rosebud's to make the necessary arrangements. Now I remember that the funeral director said some strange woman had called and asked questions.

My aunt and uncle had told me that Daddy had $650 when he came back from vacation on Sunday. *Well, okay.* The Social Security burial benefit of $250 plus that $650 was approaching the amount needed for an inexpensive funeral. The next step was to go to the police station, identify myself, and retrieve the items he had on his person, including the $650. Or so I thought.

Just as I had planned, I went to the police, identified myself, and retrieved Daddy's personal items—minus the $650. "I'm sorry, Mrs. Matthews," the officer said. "Mrs. Hamilton picked up the money." *Well, okay, whoever that is.* By now, I realized that I was in for a real fight.

"Lord, what's going on?" I asked. "Work this out."

The next step was to go to the corporate office of the department store where Daddy had worked. Sure enough, one Lula Hamilton was the first beneficiary. Tommie Matthews was the second beneficiary. *Strike two.* I still had only a grand total of $250. I thought, *well, at least I'll go to his apartment and get one of the new suits he'd recently purchased for his burial clothes.* I had no such luck. The new suits had disappeared. I settled for the best of his old suits.

Someone was a step ahead of me. Guess who?

By now, I had a permanent chauffeur. I knew very little about Oklahoma City, and I am grateful to the people who were so concerned and so helpful. Two of them were my aunt—my mother's sister—and her husband. He called an attorney friend and made an appointment for me.

In the meantime, I called my pastor and requested prayer by him and the congregation. I was becoming fatigued and mentally weary. Yes, I was praying, but I realized that I needed backup prayer. It makes good sense to call in the troops when you are taking care of business matters and doing battle with the enemy at the same time. There I was on foreign territory, totally dependent on others for transportation, listening to ideas and suggestions from others. *Yes! Help, Lord!*

I wanted to take care of all this so I could go home. However, when the time came for me to see the attorney, he gave me some information I was not ready to receive. "Mrs. Matthews," he said, "Oklahoma is one of the two states in the nation where common-law marriage is legal. The only recourse you have is to talk with the common-law wife and see what the two of you can work out."

Personally, I did not want to work on anything at all. I only wanted to go to Memphis. However, Daddy's first cousin owned a motel, and his wife knew Lula very well because she dropped by quite often. She agreed to bring Lula by to meet with me. Sure enough, she did just that.

I went outside and sat in the backseat of the car. Lula sat in the front seat with the driver. She proceeded to tell me that she remembered me from my 1974 visit to Oklahoma City. In fact, she was the friend who was with Daddy the last day I saw him alive.

When she had finished, I proceeded to tell her why I was there. "Lula," I said, "I'm here for one reason and one reason only. I received a call informing me that my daddy was found dead and that I needed to come and make the necessary arrangements for the burial. I'm here for no other reason. In addition, Lula, there are two things you must know about me. Number one: I'm saved. Number two: I have a good job, so I'm not looking for a handout. Besides that, I'll go home and leave you with this mess."

In spite of her present state, her conversation gave evidence of intelligence and astuteness in business. By now, we trusted each other and spoke comfortably together. Lula expressed her desire to carry Daddy's body to a small, rural Oklahoma town for burial, and I immediately said no. I assume the small town must have been her hometown.

She then went to plan B. "If you agree to move his body from Rosebud Funeral Home to Matt's Funeral Home, I will handle everything from a financial standpoint and bury him in one of his nice suits. In fact, I'll go tomorrow and take care of everything."

I believed and trusted her to do what she promised. For some reason, she just did not like Rosebud Funeral Home. So now I had to talk to both funeral directors and let Rosebud know that Matt would be taking care of everything.

Time was of essence because relatives were coming from other cities. It was Thursday, and the funeral was planned for Friday. Things were so entangled that my aunt called my mother and told her she needed to come to Oklahoma City to support me. My mother did not hesitate to come.

I was relieved, for the burden of the entire situation was lifted from me. One of the wisest decisions I made during this ordeal was to stop and let Lula handle everything. I made no suggestion for anything, not even the color of the casket.

Friday came, and I could not wait to call Matt's Funeral Home to see how things were going. To my surprise, the funeral director had not seen Lula, nor had he heard from her. *Oh my goodness, what happened? I really trusted her to do what she said.*

I do not remember how many calls I placed to Matt, but Lula never showed up there. Maybe the Holy Spirit quickened me to call Rosebud because that is what I did.

Sure enough, the Lord touched Lula's heart. In a state of drunkenness, she paid the bill at Rosebud and took a floral arrangement and a very nice suit for his burial. Of course, it was the day of the funeral, and relatives had arrived from other cities. I did not know if there would be a funeral or not. They barely had time to get the gravesite prepared.

Praise God! I got just what I wanted from the Lord.

In all fairness to Lula, I believe she was only trying to protect her rights as a wife. She did not realize she was fighting needlessly because she didn't have an opponent.

Had we not saturated Daddy's funeral arrangements with prayer, tempers could have flared. But we committed the situation to the Lord and permitted Him to untangle it. Giving all praise to God, I parted from Lula on very friendly terms.

> With men this is impossible; but with God all things are possible.
>
> —MATTHEW 19:26

Chapter 10

Anthony

M Y DAUGHTER MET Anthony Smith through his older brother Ronnie. Anthony and Ronnie were originally from Toledo, Ohio, before Ronnie moved to Atlanta, Georgia. Anthony moved to Georgia several years later.

Both Nataline and Anthony attended Cathedral of Faith Church of God in Christ, in Atlanta. After a particular Sunday morning worship service, just the two of them fellowshiped. During their conversation, Nataline causally said, "Anthony, the next time you go to Mississippi to visit your grandmother, why don't you stop in Memphis to see my mother?"

I did not know Anthony or Ronnie, but it was not the first time someone had volunteered another person to visit my home. It still happens quite often.

Eight days later, Ronnie and Anthony left for Corinth, Mississippi. They had driven several hundred miles when they were involved in a head-on collision with another vehicle. Sadly, Ronnie was killed instantly. Anthony was thrown through the windshield and landed in the middle of the highway some sixty feet from the site of the impact.

Anthony, along with Ronnie's body, was airlifted to the Regional Medical Center in Memphis. This is where I entered the picture.

After Nataline received news about the tragic accident, she called and told me what had transpired. She asked me to locate Anthony and pray for him.

The day of my initial visit to Anthony was one of the times he needed me most. He was so grateful for my presence because it was the day of Ronnie's funeral. Anthony was alone, in a hospital, in a strange city. His body was broken and bruised, and no family member or friend was present. I believe the Lord sent me on that particular day. Praise God!

His family, of course, had spent some time in Memphis after the accident, but obviously they had to go back to Ohio to make arrangements for Ronnie's funeral. I was so thankful that I was there with him. Oh, how my heart broke for him!

The accident occurred in May. Except for testing, he lay in bed for two weeks, from the second Monday in May until the fourth Sunday in May. After I left church that fourth Sunday afternoon—the day before Memorial Day—I went to the hospital to check on my new son. I had no idea that they were going to have him sit in a chair for the very first time since the accident.

I will always remember what I saw that day. Because his pelvis was broken, he sat there with a metal rod extending across his body. It reached from one side of the pelvis to the other. His bottom could not rest on the pad of the chair because the rod rested on the arms of the chair. What a sight! His countenance depicted the agony he was experiencing because of the awkward but necessary position of his body. I did not know what to do.

But out of my mouth came these words, "Lord, a spirit of slumber, a spirit of slumber." I was desperate. Right before my eyes, Anthony fell asleep, in spite of the pain that he was suffering. I am sure that I was more relieved than he was. *Praise God! Praise God!* Even as I write, I weep because of what I beheld that Sunday afternoon.

Of course, I was aware of the fact that he was expecting visitors from Atlanta the next day. That Memorial Day, when I thought the young ladies had arrived, I called the hospital. One of the girls answered the phone. I introduced myself, and we exchanged the appropriate greetings. Before our conversation ended, she informed me that they were fine, however, they were having a problem staying awake in the room. I knew why.

The spirit of slumber was present. Not only was the spirit of slumber there, but most importantly, the Spirit of God was in Anthony's room.

Before the accident, Anthony did not know the Lord as Savior. He later told me that as he lay on the highway, his body broken and bruised, he repented of his sins. After he was placed in a hospital bed, a nurse also ministered Jesus to him. At the time of this writing, he is in love with Jesus. And God uses his testimony to bless the body of Christ.

Chapter 11

Joe

~~~~~~~~

I AM CONVINCED THAT our places of employment are some of the most accessible mission fields we as Christians will ever encounter. One reason is that we usually spend at least forty hours a week in proximity to the same people. In many instances, we work with the same individuals for years.

I met Joe for the first time in 1961, when I went to work for the University of Tennessee. Joe and I were employed by the medical examiner. He worked in the county morgue, and I worked in the laboratory. Our paths crossed often, but at the time we did not really know each other.

Years later, our paths crossed again in another job setting. I worked in a chemistry laboratory, and he worked in another one that was located just across the hall from me. I cannot count the times I passed Joe in the hall with the usual greeting, "Hello Joe." Sometimes we would stop to chat, especially about people we had both known at the university.

One morning, his response to my greeting was, "Good morning, Tommie. Will you pray that I get my car back?" He explained that when he had gone outside to leave for work, his car was nowhere in sight. Naturally, he assumed that it had been stolen. I assured him that I would intercede on his behalf. I did not wait until my usual prayer time. As I walked away, I simply said, "Lord, give Joe his car back."

The effectual fervent prayer of a righteous man availeth much.

—JAMES 5:16

Several weeks passed before we bumped into each other again. My immediate question was "Joe, what happened to your car?" He gave me an answer that reflected Jesus' words:

> With men this is impossible; but with God all things are possible.
>
> —MATTHEW 19:26

He said, "On the day the car disappeared, I called a friend to come and pick me up from work. When he told his wife that he was picking me up from work because my car had disappeared, she said, 'I saw Joe's car heading for the expressway this morning.'" Evidently it never occurred to her that Joe would not be the one driving it.

Joe continued, "We decided to drive the same expressway in search of my car. We drove and drove and drove, and there was no sign of my car." In eight to nine hours, of course, the car could have been driven over five hundred miles.

"Finally I saw a car," he proceeded, "not my car, but *a* car. I said to my friend, 'Follow that car.' He did just that. After a while, the driver of the car suspected that he was being followed and pulled into a service station. We pulled in behind him."

Joe told the man they were looking for his car and gave him a vivid description of it. To Joe's surprise, the young man said, "I don't have the car, but I know where it is. If you will wait, I'll get it for you." A short while later he returned with the car, which was still intact.

What a testimony! Had I not prayed, "Lord, give Joe his car back," I doubt if he would have ever seen it again, especially in a recognizable form.

As I write this story, Jesus' words in Matthew 5 come to mind:

> Let your light so shine before men, that they may see your good works, and glorify your Father which is in heaven.
>
> —MATTHEW 5:16

Joe asked me to pray, not only because my light was shining in the workplace, but also because he saw the good works that God accomplished through me. And the Father in heaven will receive the glory when people everywhere read this story.

Chapter 12

Laura: She Is Now Convinced That Prayer Works

IT AMAZES ME how people know where to turn in times of trouble. The chief of sinners in any environment knows who can get a prayer answered. I have had people walk by me on a daily basis and barely say hello. But when a crisis arose in their lives, they sought me out.

Laura, however, did not fall into that category. She had a hearty hello almost every time she saw me, and that happened to be several times a day. Laura was in and out of my work area in the laboratory because she distributed the patients' specimens. One day, following her loud "Hello Tommie," she continued, "Tommie, I wrecked my car. Will you please pray that the Lord will bless me with a car?"

"Sure I will, Laura," I said. Immediately I prayed that the Lord would open a door through which Laura would get a car. She was a single parent who worked another job in addition to her employment at the workplace we shared. She needed transportation, and she needed it quickly.

Within a short while, Laura approached me with yet another situation. "Tommie," she said, "my insurance company sent me a check to pay my car off. But for some reason, they left the name of the lien holder off the check. I could just go on and cash this check and buy me another car."

I reminded her that I had asked the Lord to bless her with another car. "Laura," I replied, "that's not the right thing to do. Do what's right, and God will bless you. Cash the check and pay for the wrecked car."

"Well, OK," she said. "If you say so."

38

Of course, I had no doubt that she really knew what she should do. She just needed one person who would tell her that it was okay to do what she pleased with the money from the insurance company. She had hoped that I would be that one person, and that would have settled the whole matter. Well, a few days later, Laura was back. This time, the girl was all smiles. She was simply elated.

She had decided to go to Mississippi to see the car dealer from whom she had purchased her previous car. Sure enough, as she drove up, the gentleman who had helped her before recognized her. Laura explained her situation. To her surprise, the man said to her, "I'll tell you what to do. Choose any car you would like from this lot. You can name your down payment, and besides that, you may determine the amount of your monthly payment. I will accept whatever amounts you declare."

Laura said that she gave him the amount of money left over after she paid the other car off—as a down payment. She set her monthly note at $150.

To this day, Laura is convinced that prayer works. It pays to do the right thing in every situation. God does not need our help. He has already determined how He will answer our prayers.

> Now unto him that is able to do exceeding abundantly above all that we ask or think, according to the power that worketh in us.
>
> —Ephesians 3:20

Laura has blessed many with the words of her testimony.

Chapter 13

Father and Son

IT IS A never-ending story, the tale of an innocent child who is hurt because his parents separate. And so it is with little James Jr., whose parents have been divorced for several years now.

His mother has legal custody of him, but he loves both parents very, very much. His mother lives in California and his daddy lives in Tennessee. He attends school in Los Angeles and spends the summer with his daddy in Memphis.

His father said that when he picked him up at the airport in June 1997, James Jr. immediately began pleading to remain in Memphis rather than return to California in September. The child described unpleasant experiences both at home and at school. He had a real problem with his mom's live-in boyfriend. The male friend was kind to him, but according to his story, he saw and heard far too much.

The father listened to his son's story, and he was aware that there might have been a fraction of fabrication in the child's account. But he knew James Jr. well enough to believe that a great deal of the story was valid.

The summer months sped by all too quickly, and school was to begin soon. By now, the mother was ready for her baby to come home, and the daddy was in a terrible predicament. He decided that his only recourse was to fight for custody of the child. He talked to a lawyer who agreed to take the case for a fee of $1,000 with a down payment of $500, money he did not have.

The lawyer told the father that the case would have to go before a judge in Memphis, and three things would be necessary to gain custody. First, he would have to prove that the child was in school in Memphis. Second, it would be important to show a pattern of abuse. Third, he needed a deposition from a noted child psychologist.

The father did not have $500, but he knew a child psychologist and made an appointment for his son to see her. After the examination, the teary-eyed psychologist was obviously upset and told the father that the child should by no means be allowed to return to California. She told him that his son's sense of well-being and love rested with him and that he should keep James Jr. with him.

He now possessed the required deposition from a child psychologist. The very same day, he boldly enrolled him in school. Not only that, but he also secured the necessary $500 to pay the lawyer. He felt as if he was really on a roll.

There was one small problem. He could not find the lawyer. He called and called her, but she did not answer, and she didn't return his call. While all this was happening in Memphis, an excited mother in California was anxiously awaiting the arrival of her son. She had been given the necessary flight information so she could be at the airport to meet him.

When I saw the daddy on the church's parking lot, he related this story to me. He ended it by saying that he had enrolled his son in school here although the boy's packed bags were in the trunk of his car. As a matter of fact, I saw the boy's bags.

But the time had come for him to make a telephone call to California, and inform the mother of little James that he would not be on the scheduled flight. Oh, how he dreaded it! I served a twofold purpose. I listened, and as I walked off, I prayed, "Lord, touch the heart of little James's mother so that she agrees with what has happened in Memphis."

I do not remember all of the details, but I do remember what happened when I saw the little fellow again. His face was all smiles as he jumped into my arms and exclaimed, "Thanks for praying for me!"

Later his father explained what had happened. When he called the mother and told her that the child was already attending school in Memphis, she only said, "Well, OK. I would probably have done the same thing had the situation been reversed."

Praise God! After hearing this story, I knew I could not unscramble the mix-up. But I knew who could, and He did just that.

Yes, He did it again.

Chapter 14

Lord, Get Me Out of Paris

$\smile\!\!\!\sim\!\!\!\supset$

T ERRY, NATALINE, ELEANOR, and I planned a trip to
Paris in December 1993. I was very excited, but several
days before our scheduled departure, my aunt in Dallas
became critically ill. She was immediately rushed to the hospital
and placed on a respirator.

Ours was an unusual aunt-niece relationship. Aunt Billie was
ten years old when I was born, and from the beginning, I am told,
she thought and acted as if I were her baby. Through the years,
she had assumed the roles of aunt, sister, and mother to me. She
did an equally outstanding job in each of these roles.

Needless to say, thoughts of Paris no longer excited me after
I received the disturbing telephone calls from Dallas. I was in a
dilemma, to say the least. We attempted to find someone who
would purchase my ticket and go in my stead. Of course, we
could not find anyone who was interested in going or who could
afford to go. Many calls crossed the wires between Memphis and
Dallas in a short period of time. All the while, I was praying,
Lord, what must I do?

The decision to go was made when Billy—my aunt's eldest
son, who also served as her pastor—insisted that I go on the trip.
Eleanor and I departed Memphis for Atlanta on the morning of
December 9, 1993. We met Nataline and Terry at the Atlanta
airport, and we all departed for France that afternoon.

The four of us arrived at Orly Airport at four o'clock in the
morning, Paris time. It was a dreary, foggy, Friday morning. By
the time our taxi delivered us to our hotel, we were ready for bed.

We slept until early afternoon and then dressed and took to the streets of Paris.

It was an exciting stroll, and we acted like four teenagers. Even so, I was still trying to remove Dallas and my aunt's critical condition from my thoughts. The next day we went on a sightseeing tour, and the sights were awesome. It was as if the pictures from my high school world history book had leaped from the pages before my very eyes.

On Sunday, we received the call came from Memphis. Aunt Billie did not make it. Someone told me later that she was pronounced dead by the time we reached New York City from Atlanta. I suppose that my family was gracious enough to withhold the news from me as long as they possibly could. However, they could not wait any longer because I had to leave Paris on Monday to be at the funeral in Dallas on Tuesday.

Our departure was scheduled for Thursday, which meant that I would miss seeing many of the sights. But the Lord worked for us on Sunday evening. He touched a cab driver and gave him a heart to take all four of us to the places of our choosing for a price of fifty American dollars.

We saw the Eiffel Tower at night. What a splendor! We visited the Cathedral of Notre Dame, where Mass was in progress. Then he drove us to Versailles, which is located twelve miles southwest of Paris. I would not have seen much more had I stayed until Thursday.

By Monday, I was packed and set to leave for Dallas. I did not know what to expect at the airport, but I knew that God had to intervene. A clause on the ticket stated that a monetary penalty would be imposed if a ticket holder violated the contractual terms.

I did know that another ticket would have to be purchased. The second part of my original round-trip would be invalid. Under these circumstances, a ticket from Paris to Dallas was $1,300, and a ticket from Paris to Atlanta was $1,100. The purchase of another ticket was out of the question.

Thank God for our friend Kathy, who was communicating with the travel agency in Atlanta on my behalf. She, in turn, was faxing the information to me.

The other three members of my traveling party accompanied

me to the airport on Monday morning. I prayed all the way there. One thing I said was "Lord, lead me to the person you have chosen to assist me when I go to the ticket counter."

When I arrived at the counter, a very cordial young lady approached me and asked, "May I help you?" I explained that I had to leave the country because of a death in my family, and she checked the computer and quoted me a price of $100 for a flight from Paris to Atlanta. I had a credit card in hand.

Before she processed the card, however, I saw a distinct change in her facial expression. She consulted several other agents before returning to where I was standing. Apologetically, she said, "Ma'am, I'm so sorry, but you purchased a special ticket, which stipulates that you must remain here for a seven-day period."

I was very much aware of the clause. Even more so, I knew that I had prayed, and prayer eliminates clauses. My next step was to go to her superior. She sought the advice of a middle-aged gentleman, who immediately advised her to let the $100 quote stand. Praise the Lord! I was off to Atlanta for a fare of $100.

> And whatsoever ye shall ask in my name, that will I do, that the Father may be glorified in the Son. If ye shall ask any thing in my name, I will do it.
>
> —JOHN 14:13–14

When I arrived in Atlanta, I purchased another ticket. The cost of the ticket from Atlanta to Dallas was $360. I paid for the ticket, and as I turned to walk away from the counter, the agent asked if I had arrived on an international flight. She told me that if that was the case, she had overcharged me, and I was due a refund.

As you see, the Lord continued to work on my behalf. I arrived in Dallas on Monday night. In fact, I made it to the funeral home in time for the wake. The Lord comforted us during trying times, as I knew He would. We were consoled by the fact that Aunt Billie was with the Lord.

> Precious in the sight of the LORD is the death of his saints.
>
> —PSALM 116:15

Chapter 15

Valujet

⟨～～～⟩

I WAS DELIGHTED WHEN Valujet Airlines began services between Memphis and Atlanta in 1993. It meant that I could visit my daughter with a day's notice and a reasonable fare. The cost of a round-trip ticket exceeded that of driving my car by only a few dollars. Needless to say, I could not even begin to place a monetary value on the advantage of a one-hour flight over an exhausting seven-hour drive.

It got better. My son, Marvin, and his family moved to Clearwater, Florida, just across the bay from Tampa. Valujet services also existed between Memphis and Tampa. This time we were comparing a fifteen-hour drive to a two-hour flight. I was doubly blessed. A mother likes to know that she has quick access to her children without having to pay a fortune.

But then, on May 11, 1996, Valujet flight number 555 from Miami to Atlanta crashed in the Florida Everglades, with no survivors. I thought that the tragedy meant the end of the quick, inexpensive means of reaching my children. *I would rather drive any day,* I reasoned. Isn't it something how outward circumstances change our mental outlook? Mine changed as soon as I heard the news bulletin about the crash.

After a thorough investigation by the national governing body of airlines and compliance by Valujet, services were restored. Most of my doubts—but not all of them—subsided after a while. So I began to consult the Lord and ask Him if I was to fly again.

One Wednesday night, the Bible study topic was "Have Faith in God." As the pastor spoke, I prayed, *Lord, should I fly Valujet?*

46

It was then that the discussion turned specifically to Valujet. The pastor said, "It seems that the airline crash was due to an explosion caused by cylinders that were not emptied before they were placed on the plane. The crash was definitely caused by human error." He then continued, "I said that for your benefit, Evangelist Matthews."

Of course, I already knew the news account of the cylinders that should not have been placed on the plane. But this time, the words had been spoken to me through the pastor in answer to my prayer. In essence, the Lord said, "Yes, it's okay to fly Valujet."

Thank you, Lord. I booked a flight to Atlanta shortly thereafter.

> I will bless the LORD, who hath given me counsel: my reins also instruct me in the night seasons.
>
> —PSALM 16:7

Chapter 16

Datsun or Marquis?

I LOVED THE MERCURY Marquis automobile. By the time my son graduated from high school, I was driving my second Marquis. Of course, I was having second thoughts because it was rather large. When you have two children in college at the same time, it is natural to look for ways to save money.

So I began to think of the money I could save on gas alone if I traded my car for a much smaller one. *Maybe I'll just buy a Datsun,* I thought. To this day, I do not know why I concentrated on the purchase of a Datsun when there were other small cars on the market.

Anyway, I consulted my Source. "Lord, should I buy a Datsun, or do I keep my car?" I asked. I did not get an immediate answer, but I continued asking.

One day, instead of going to lunch with my usual lunch buddies, I decided to go alone. As I entered the elevator, I joined four adults who were already riding it. When the door closed, they continued their conversation.

One man said to another, "Listen, if you buy a Datsun, you'll pay the price in parts." He continued, "An alternator costs $118, so you might as well keep the Marquis."

Thank you, Lord, for encouraging me to go to lunch alone that particular day. Had I gone with the usual gang, I would have missed the answer to my prayer.

> And this is the confidence that we have in him, that, if we ask any thing according to his will, he heareth us: And if we know that he hear us, whatsoever we ask, we know that we have the petitions that we desired of him.
> —1 JOHN 5:14–15

Chapter 17

Lord, Give Me a New Mercedes

⟶

PRIOR TO 1988, I owned three new cars: a 1962 Ford, 1969 Mercury, and 1977 Mercury. As you can see, a new car was *not* on my shopping list every three years. I drove a car as long as it took me where I wanted to go.

Surprisingly, after I bought my new car in 1977, I decided that my next car purchase would be a Mercedes-Benz. But when I needed another car in 1983, I thought, *not a Mercedes-Benz just yet.* Talk is easy, and it's cheap. However, I still did not want to purchase a new car of another make because I truly felt that it was just a matter of time before the big purchase.

So I began to search the daily newspaper, as well as the weekly shopper, for what I called an interim car. Finally, I spotted an ad for the sale of three cars and visited the very nice middle-aged couple who had placed it. They were preparing to leave Memphis to return to their native land of Greece.

After looking at all three cars, I purchased a Ford Maverick from them. I intended to drive it only a few months until I was fully persuaded to spend in excess of $30,000 for an automobile. However, I soon discovered that I had made a very wise purchase because of the service rendered by the Maverick. In addition, the couple returned to Memphis because of their dissatisfaction with Greece and asked to buy the car back from me. Needless to say, I declined their offer.

The car was super. I drove it one year, two years, three years, and four years. Yet, even I knew the car would not last forever, although I hoped it would. In the meantime, I began to confess my new Mercedes-Benz. People who knew me well listened attentively. Some of them believed with me, but not everyone

49

did. Of course, what others believed was not the key; what I believed was important.

> Therefore I say unto you, What things soever ye desire, when ye pray, believe that ye receive them, and ye shall have them.
>
> —MARK 11:24

I believed. In the words of a twentieth century comedian, "What you see is what you get." But I say, what the Lord says is what you get. What does He say?

> Beloved, I wish above all things that thou mayest prosper and be in health, even as thy soul prospereth.
>
> —3 JOHN 2

God wants to bless us. Oh yes! He does! He wants the whole man to prosper and be blessed.

> Delight thyself also in the LORD; and he shall give thee the desires of thine heart.
>
> —PSALM 37:4

Not only will God give us the desires of our hearts, but I also believe that as we delight ourselves in Him, He places desires in our hearts. I believe that my Heavenly Father desired that I would own a nice car, and therefore, He placed the desire in my heart. With this desire, I began to study the Mercedes-Benz. And I lived just five minutes from the only Mercedes-Benz dealership in the city.

Time after time, I visited the dealership and picked up brochures to read and study makes and models for an idea of the car I wanted. The salespeople were not exactly running over each other to assist me, and I cannot say that I blamed them. My after-work appearance did leave something to be desired and maybe questioned. "I'll own one of these one day," I confessed to the car dealer as I toured the showroom on one of my visits. Can't you hear him saying, "Yeah, right"?

By now, I was confessing, looking, and studying. I was not yet buying because my little secondhand car was running well. But isn't it something how the Lord permits circumstances to occur in our lives so that we may be blessed?

March 9, 1988. "This is the day which the LORD hath made; we will rejoice and be glad in it" (Psalm 118:24). Like I had done many other days, I ran an errand during my lunch hour. Guess what? As I drove from the parking lot and prepared to make a left turn onto the street, my car was hit and totaled by an oncoming Corvette.

The time had come to purchase the new car. I realized that so much had to be done. The first step was to go to the bank and apply for a loan. I could no longer procrastinate because I desperately needed my own transportation, not that of other people. By this time, I knew that I desired a black 260E Mercedes-Benz. However, the local dealership had no such car.

A friend searched for a black car in Atlanta, and a relative checked in the Dallas-Fort Worth area. My cousin in Dallas secured a broker, who looked in Florida and probably other states. When they could not locate the car I desired, I knew it was time to check with the Source—the all-wise, ever-present, all-knowing God.

"Okay, Lord. Where is the car?" I asked.

After I prayed, I felt in my spirit that it was in Texas. Many times, the Lord answers our prayers in what I have called "bits and pieces." I believe this process is a test to see if we are going to persist or give up. He loves the communion with His children.

> In all thy ways acknowledge him, and he shall direct thy paths.
>
> —PROVERBS 3:6

Texas, huh? Okay, Texas, here I come.

Saturday afternoon, May 13, 1988, I boarded a plane for Dallas. While my cousin and I drove from the DFW airport to where I would be staying, we decided to check the one Dallas dealership that he had not already checked.

I will never forget the words of the middle-aged dealer when I inquired about the car of my choice. "If you have come in asking for a black 260E," he said, "you have done your homework. That's our best kept secret." His statement referred to the fact that the

260E was a smaller version of the 300E, the highly advertised and more expensive model.

He also informed me that the black car was in high demand and very hard to keep on the floor. *Oh well, it's not here either*, I thought. Now I wonder how, when the Lord said Texas, I decided on my own that it was in Dallas. He did not say Dallas, Texas. He placed Texas within my spirit, with no mention of a town or city.

As I lay in bed that Saturday night, I asked God again, "Lord, where is the car? I'm in Texas, and this is a big, big state, You know. This is where I grew up." That same night I received a call from my son, Marvin, and his wife, Carol, who lived in Tyler, Texas, approximately one hundred miles from Dallas.

"Little Momma, why don't you come to Tyler on Sunday?" Carol asked. "We'll come to Dallas to get you after church, and we will be sure to get you back to Dallas on Monday." After much persuasion on their part, I finally gave in. Carol and a friend came for me on Sunday, and I left reluctantly for Tyler, of all places.

On Monday morning, Carol said, "We have a Mercedes dealership in Tyler. Let's stop in." We drove onto the lot, and out walked a young man. "Sir, do you have a 260E Mercedes-Benz?" I asked.

"Yes, we do," he replied. "I'm not the Mercedes dealer, but I'll show it to you." There it was at the front of the lot, the black 260E Mercedes-Benz.

The negotiations began. The more I disagreed with the quote, the more he dropped the price. Why were they lowering the price to sell the car to me? I knew why. This was happening according to God's plan. He, as my Representative, was in control.

We negotiated for hours on Monday. Finally, I called it off. "I'll be back tomorrow," I said. He all but panicked, asking me to promise to come back on Tuesday. I did promise, but I wanted to make just one more call to be sure there was not another car of my choosing for a lower price. My Dallas contact was still checking, and I had to be sure that he had not located a car.

By Tuesday morning, I knew that this was the purchase I was to make. This was my car. The necessary business call was placed to my bank in Memphis, and it was done. The case was closed.

The lady who handled the paperwork and closed the business transaction said to me, "I have never seen anyone come in and leave with a deal like you have." It was amazing how everything worked in my favor. It was time to go home.

The salesman gave me a crash course on driving my new car. In other words, he taught me how to use the buttons and knobs so I could drive without any problems. As I got into the car, I gave him a brand new gospel tract that I had purchased before I left Memphis. I already knew that he was not a Christian because I had asked him during our negotiations. "My mother is a Christian much like you," he had said. "She is praying for me."

We said good-bye, and I drove off, highly blessed of the Lord because I saw Him in the midst of the negotiations. I thought about the salesman as I drove to Memphis and also after I returned home. He was so kind. I remembered how the love of God moved upon my heart the first time I saw him.

As I left for church on Thursday evening two weeks later, I went to the mailbox because I had not checked the mail during the day. *Just an advertisement*, I thought, as I noticed a business envelope. I decided to leave it in the box and read it later.

When I returned from church, I opened the envelope postmarked Tyler, Texas. To my surprise, a handwritten letter was inside, not the expected typewritten information associated with a business advertisement. The note read:

> *Dear Mrs. Matthews,*
>
> *I hope you are enjoying your new car. I just want you to know that God has won another victory—me. After going through one of the most difficult situations in my life, I have received the Lord as Savior. Please let me know the next time you are in Tyler, and we'll go to church together.*

I cannot begin to tell anyone how I felt. Joy flooded my soul. I screamed. I shouted right on my front porch at ten o'clock at night.

QUESTIONS

- Why didn't the dealership in Memphis, just five minutes from my house, have the car of my choice?

- Why wasn't the car in the Dallas-Fort Worth area, where there are many dealerships?

- Why did I have to purchase an airline ticket to Dallas? Why could I not refuse to go to Tyler?

- Why was the Mercedes dealer not available to show me the car that morning?

- Why was the young man who walked outside when I drove up not the salesman ?

ANSWERS

- God is sovereign, and He can do whatever He wants to do whenever He wants to.

- It was *not* about a black 260E Mercedes-Benz, but it *was* about the salesman who received my witness for Christ.

Chapter 18

Cover My Car With Your Blood

A s I APPROACHED my car to leave for work, I was tired, sleepy, and anxiously awaiting the weekend. Out of my spirit came the words, *Lord, cover my car with Your blood.* I am a person who likes quiet in the morning, and I prefer to not talk to anyone unless it is absolutely necessary.

The weekend came and, as usual, Saturday was a day of shopping, cleaning, and running errands. It was a bright, sunshiny day. While I was out, I decided to go to the service station and fill my car with gasoline. As a creature of habit, I drove to Pump 8 and aligned the gas tank with the pump, pointing my car toward a very busy intersection. Then I ran inside and yelled, "Fill me up on 8." This, of course, was part of my routine, and I had done it many times before—same station, same pump. It took all of ten seconds or less.

By the time I had returned to pump the gasoline, the car had disappeared. I could not imagine what had happened in such a short period of time. After I regained my composure, I realized that the alarm I was hearing was coming from my car. I turned in the direction of the sound, and to my surprise, the car was headed directly into the street. The north-and-south stoplight was green, which meant that cars going against the path of my car had the right of way.

I will never forget what I saw that bright June day. It was if my car was graciously maneuvered out of the path of oncoming traffic. What a sight! All I could say was, "Lord, save my car." When it was out of the path of traffic, two young men managed to bring it to a halt. One of them hopped into the car, and the other one stood in front of it and braced himself against it. People were watching in sheer amazement.

To this very day, I shudder to think what would have happened had the Spirit of the Lord not released from my spirit the prayer, "Lord, cover my car with Your blood." The possibilities were many—car wrecks, pileups, injuries, lawsuits, and death.

I had just completed Benny Hinn's book *The Blood*. Praise God for it! Through this powerful work, I was reminded of the power in the blood of Jesus Christ.

Benny Hinn said, "There is no question about the power in the blood of Jesus. At the same time, the blood does not have magical powers by itself. The power comes from the Lord Jesus Himself, and He is the One who will act on our behalf when we apply His blood through prayer. It is the Lord who covers us; we do not cover ourselves."[1]

In his book, *The Power of the Blood*, Pastor Maxwell Whyte tells how he and his family experienced the protection of the blood of Jesus as they lived in England during World War II.[2]

> We went through many dangerous air raids when buzz bombs were flying elsewhere. But we were able to lie down with our children and sleep through much of it. The protection of the blood of Jesus was so real that it seemed liked we were sleeping in a strong shelter. In fact, we used to speak of the blood as the best air raid shelter in the world.

Pastor Whyte said that they would ask the Lord to cover them, their home, and their children with the blood every night before they went to sleep. One night, thirteen bombs landed within three-quarters of a mile of their home. Aside from some minor damage to the house, they were all kept safe. I remember how he told our congregation again and again that he had never known the active, audible pleading of the blood to fail.

R. A. Torrey says:

> We must know the power of the blood if we are to know the power of God. Our knowing experimentally the

power of the Word, the power of the Holy Spirit, and the power of prayer is dependent upon our knowing the power of the blood of Christ.[3]

Praise God for the blood of Christ. Thank Him for the blood.

Chapter 19

When God Says,
"Too Much"—It's Too Much

⌒

O NCE AGAIN, I had taken on too many projects at one time. If I was not doing something, I was thinking about it. I have discovered that thinking about a project is much worse than the actual performance of it. Somehow, for reasons I do not understand, my undertakings become magnified. The longer they are in process, the bigger they become. It is like inviting guests for dinner and continuing to clean or cook until they arrive.

This attribute did not come from the Holy Spirit. I have always possessed this "magnification factor," as I call it. As a high school student, I wore myself out by making every effort to do the very best when I participated in an activity. It might have been a literary event like a spelling or essay contest or sports competition in basketball or tennis. It did not matter; we had to win. The track coach wanted to use me on the track team, not because I could run so fast, but because I ran so hard.

My grandmother would sometimes become very aggravated when I arrived home several hours after school had ended, so tired I would almost drop. Her famous last words were "Can't they find someone else to do that?" I guess she did not know that I was doing exactly what I wanted to do—to simply do everything within my power to make my school the best in its category.

Well, anyway, forty-three years later, the magnification factor still exists. As I stated before, I knew that my hands were moving in too many directions, and the Holy Spirit bore witness by putting an all-too-familiar check in my spirit.

As I sat in the worship service one Sunday morning, I began to talk to the Lord about what I was doing and the heaviness in my spirit. While I was talking to Him, He answered me through a note a church elder passed me. It was directly from the Holy Spirit and read, *"Evangelist, the Lord said, 'Free yourself—too much."* As soon as I read the note, the heaviness in my chest lifted.

In obedience to the voice of the Holy Spirit, I departed the very next day for a week of rest and meditation. I have no desire of becoming another Epaphroditus, who gambled with his life in rendering service to Christ.

> Yet I supposed it necessary to send to you Epaphroditus, my brother, and companion in labour, and fellowsoldier, but your messenger, and he that ministered to my wants. For he longed after you all, and was full of heaviness, because that ye had heard that he had been sick. For indeed he was sick nigh unto death: but God had mercy on him; and not on him only, but on me also, lest I should have sorrow upon sorrow. I sent him therefore the more carefully, that, when ye see him again, ye may rejoice, and that I may be the less sorrowful. Receive him therefore in the Lord with all gladness; and hold such in reputation: because for the work of Christ he was nigh unto death, not regarding his life, to supply your lack of service toward me.
>
> —PHILIPPIANS 2:25–30

I am thankful for fellow believers who are sensitive to the Spirit's voice and are caring and bold enough to tell me what the Lord is saying. We are all indwelt by the same Holy Spirit.

> There is one body, and one Spirit, even as ye are called in one hope of your calling; One Lord, one faith, one baptism, One God and Father of all, who is above all, and through all, and in you all.
>
> —EPHESIANS 4:4–6

In addition, I am grateful to my holy Father, who is so mindful of my well-being that He stopped me before I damaged myself physically.

Chapter 20

Thou Art the Lord That Healeth Me

H OW MANY TIMES, at any sign of pain, did I reach over with my left hand and lay it on my right shoulder? After a while, I did it automatically. This went on for months. If I did not feel any discomfort, I ignored it because I believed God would heal it. Healing is provided as part of Christ's atonement.

> Who his own self bare our sins in his own body on the tree, that we, being dead to sins, should live unto righteousness: by whose stripes ye were healed.
> —1 PETER 2:24

> When the even was come, they brought unto him many that were possessed with devils: and he cast out the spirits with [his] word, and healed all that were sick: That it might be fulfilled which was spoken by Esaias the prophet, saying, Himself took our infirmities, and bare our sicknesses.
> —MATTHEW 8:16–17

In addition to me praying for myself, my pastor also prayed for me.

> Is any sick among you? let him call for the elders of the church; and let them pray over him, anointing him with oil in the name of the Lord: And the prayer of faith shall save the sick, and the Lord shall raise him up; and if he have committed sins, they shall be forgiven him.
> —JAMES 5:14–15

Since there was no visible, physical change in my arm, I went to the Source. I went to the One who made my arm. "Lord, what are you going to do about my arm?" I asked. He took me directly to the Word of God and spoke to me:

> Then Jesus answered and said unto her, O woman, great is thy faith: be it unto thee even as thou wilt. And her daughter was made whole from that very hour.
> —MATTHEW 15:28

After I read that scripture, I knew I had faith sufficient for the healing of my arm. By this time, my arm was immobile in the shoulder area. It was impossible for me to raise it. As a matter of fact, I had to place my left arm all the way across my head to comb the right side of my hair. I soon realized that my shoulder was frozen. My next question was "Lord, where do I go from here?"

> Then shall we know, if we follow on to know the LORD.
> —HOSEA 6:3

It was evident that the Lord wanted to teach me a new truth about the art of healing as I followed on to know Him.

In response to the question I asked Him, God led me to our laboratory director. I told him about my upper right arm, and he in turn referred me to an orthopedics specialist. I took the director's advice, and within a few days I met with Dr. John. He did a thorough examination of my arm and confirmed that the shoulder joint was frozen. He said it one of the worst cases he had seen.

Dr. John then referred me to a physical therapist. He was hoping that the therapist's work would cause my arm to become mobile again. When I met with the therapist, she also told me the state of the arm was among the worst she had ever seen.

Oh me! I thought. I could not believe that I had permitted this to happen because of sheer negligence on my part. I was faithful to keep my appointments, and the therapist exemplified great diligence in working with me. But there was no improvement at all.

I went back to Dr. John, and he talked briefly of putting me to sleep and manipulating my arm. Then he implied that even though he could perform this procedure, it still might be ineffective. I did not like his statement of doubt because by now I strongly sensed that he was God's choice to restore my arm to its proper use. After all, the Lord had spoken directly to me from Matthew 15:28 and said, "Be it unto thee even as thou wilt." I was more than ready for my healing to be manifested.

When I recalled God's promise in His Word, I encouraged Dr. John to do the manipulation procedure. I will admit that I did not know what all was involved in it, but I did know that I wanted to be made whole. Dr. John told me that I would need to be admitted to the hospital to be prepared for one-day surgery. In summary, he said I would be wheeled into the surgery unit where I would be anesthetized, and he would move my arm as much as possible without breaking it.

My therapist warned me that I would experience terrible pain after I awakened from the manipulation process. I could not afford to entertain the thought of pain, and I immediately prayed, "Lord, you know I don't like pain." I tried to avoid thinking of anything that would cause me to be fearful. I just wanted to get it over with.

A few days after meeting with the doctor, I entered the hospital and he manipulated my arm. Thank God, I woke up with a pain-free arm that was at least 85 percent operable. After additional physical therapy treatments, more improvement was evident. Today, five years later, I can use my right arm almost as effectively as my left arm.

The Lord taught me that He is sovereign and that He does what He wants to when He wants.

> So then it is not of him that willeth, nor of him that runneth, but of God that showeth mercy.
> —ROMANS 9:16

For reasons known only to God, He chose to heal me through a process whereby He employed those trained in the field of medicine. I believe that God channeled His healing powers through medical doctors, although I had expected that I would be healed through the laying-on of hands.

...[F]or I am the LORD that healeth thee.

—EXODUS 15:26

He is Jehovah-Rapha.

Chapter 21

Don't Quit—We Will Win!

I AM CONVINCED THAT a few rotten apples do spoil the barrel. Over a thirty-year period, I worked with many people, and I observed that some are gifted in the area of causing problems for their fellow employees. In any group setting, such as family, work, or church, it seems that there are those who seek to gain favor with the leader. So it was in my workplace.

Three sections worked under one manager, Annie. I was in charge of Section A, Lottie was over Section B, and Charles was the supervisor of Section C. We three worked very well together. A few other technologists worked in all three laboratories on a rotational basis.

Two of the young ladies had once been permanent employees in my area, and how they caused confusion! It was rumored that one of them desired my position, and the other one was her friend. The aspiring leader openly criticized other employees, emphasizing their weaknesses and magnifying the severity of errors they made.

Besides all this, she reported her complaints to the manager. She took it upon herself to do what I was paid to do. It was a very difficult time for the other employees in my area and for me. I would tell them, "Don't quit because we are going to win."

The Lord gave me the courage to stand up for what was right. I found myself responding, "Oh no! We can't do that. It's not right." Or I declared, "That's not fair." My evaluation was going to be tampered with anyway. My overall rating would read *competent* instead of *commendable* or *outstanding*. So what did I have to lose?

At first, I defended myself at evaluation time by pointing out areas in which I totally disagreed. It did not work. The manager pretended to listen, but she already knew her intentions concerning me. She desired to discredit me in the eyes of my superiors, who esteemed me highly in my area of expertise. Ultimately, she hoped that I would resign so she could hire Julia as my replacement.

Her strategy worked for a moment, and the enemy, working through her, had me on the run for a short time.

> Be sober, be vigilant; because your adversary the devil, as a roaring lion, walketh about, seeking whom he may devour.
>
> —1 PETER 5:8

I began using my lunch hour to look for another job. I even called my old boss, whom I had worked for ten years before I came to the hospital. The salary he quoted me was about half my current annual salary. Well, that was out. There was no way that I could take a salary cut, considering the fact that I was the sole support of myself and two children in college.

Yes, I was praying without ceasing, but I was not listening. Finally, I stopped and analyzed the situation. Those who are willing to hire me will not pay me according to my experience, I thought. Something is wrong. I am trying to leave here, and the Lord is saying no. The Lord was blocking my exit.

All the time, the Lord was calling my name and saying:

> Fear ye not, stand still, and see the salvation of the LORD, which he will show to you to day…The LORD shall fight for you, and ye shall hold your peace.
>
> —EXODUS 14:13–14

"Yes, Lord, I hear you. Finally, I hear you. I will not leave the job that you blessed me with. This is your hospital, and you are my Father. Since I am your child, I have every right to be here. So, I am here until you say differently. Yes, Lord, I hear you. Finally, I hear you."

He was oppressed, and he was afflicted, yet he opened
not his mouth: he is brought as a lamb to the slaugh-
ter, and as a sheep before her shearers is dumb, so he
openeth not his mouth.

—Isaiah 53:7

"Yes, Lord, I understand. When I go in for the next evaluation, I'm going in as a dumb sheep before her shearers, and I
will not open my mouth." I could not wait until it was time to
be evaluated again. It was simply wonderful. Whatever Annie
said, my response was, "Okay, that's fine." Even as I write, I am
reminded:

Agree with thine adversary quickly.

—Matthew 5:25

As I agreed with my adversary, the adversary became con-
fused.Finally, the Holy Spirit gave me the words that destroyed
the yoke. We were sitting in my manager's office on another
occasion, having the usual "she said…" conversation, when
these words came out of my mouth: "Annie, you must realize
that these young ladies who work in my area see me in the role
of a nanny and not as their supervisor. As a result, they are having problems adjusting." As soon as I spoke these words, tears
filled her eyes.

And the yoke shall be destroyed because of the anointing.

—Isaiah 10:27

From that day forward, things began to change for me. Annie
now supported my decisions and actually complimented the
quality of work we turned out. This same woman, who had previ-
ously tampered with my evaluation, now permitted me to evalu-
ate myself. That was God, I guarantee you. My overall evaluation
rating was commendable, not competent.

The king's heart is in the hand of the Lord, as the rivers
of water: he turneth it whithersoever he will.

—Proverbs 21:1

Yes, God is truly amazing!

Praise God! But this was only the beginning. Please read the rest of the story.

Chapter 22

Prayer Moves the Hand of God

⟶

LTHOUGH GOD WAS moving, I kept praying, "Lord, transfer these two young ladies from my area." I realize that the enemy departs for a season. Luke wrote about what happened after the devil had tempted Jesus in the wilderness:

> And when the devil had ended all the temptation, he departed from him for a season.
>
> —LUKE 4:13

I did not trust them, and I wished them happiness elsewhere. Enough was enough. Never once did I wish them ill will or hope that they would lose their jobs. No, no, that's not God's way.

> Rejoice not when thine enemy falleth, and let not thine heart be glad when he stumbleth: Lest the LORD see it, and it displease him, and he turn away his wrath from him.
>
> —PROVERBS 24:17–18

> Pray without ceasing.
>
> —1 THESSALONIANS 5:17

I adhered to the above scripture. I prayed without ceasing, "Lord, transfer them from my area."

In chapter 21, I described the laboratory setting. Remember, we had only one manager over three distinct sections:

68

Section A	Tommie
Section B	Lottie
Section C	Charles

The day finally came when my prayer was answered. The young ladies were transferred to Charles's section, and the climate in my area became wonderful. There was such a freedom, and we all enjoyed coming to work again. I was so happy for the others who worked with me. They had gone through so much adversity based on lies. Their motives were pure, and they were also excellent technologists and loyal employees.

As time passed, I assumed that the other two sections had stabilized and things were going along smoothly for everyone. As I passed the manager's office one day, I heard an all-too-familiar voice, tattling and stirring up trouble for Charles's section. "Oh no," I said, "surely not her again."

The enemy was employing the same tactics. I think I experienced a flashback to my previous struggles because I prayed with a wrong attitude. "Lord," I said, "now you are going to have to do something about this. She's still making trouble for the employees in the other area. It isn't right."

Sometimes I pray and forget that I have spoken to the Lord about my concerns. So it was in this instance.

> Casting all your cares upon him; for he careth for you.
> —1 PETER 5:7

I whispered my prayer as I worked. A few days later, I heard an all-important rumor. The word through the grapevine was that Charles's section was going to become an independent area, no longer part of the present workplace structure. This would be especially good news for Charles because he would now be promoted to manager. Interesting enough, I thought, but is it true?

Well, I knew whom to ask. As I sat in the chapel, I said, "Lord, I heard that Section C is going is going to become a separate setup with Charles as manager. Is it true?"

Immediately, the Lord responded, "Yes, it's true because you prayed."

> For the eyes of the Lord are over the righteous, and his ears are open unto their prayers: but the face of the Lord is against them that do evil.
>
> —1 PETER 3:12

> The sacrifice of the wicked is an abomination to the LORD: but the prayer of the upright is his delight.
>
> —PROVERBS 15:8

> The LORD is far from the wicked: but he heareth the prayer of the righteous.
>
> —PROVERBS 15:29

Very shortly afterwards, Section C became an independent area. To this day, Charles does not realize how the organizational change and his promotion came about. However, God knows—and I know.

Prayer moves the hand of God.

Chapter 23

It's Not Over Until It's Over

B Y NOW, THINGS were going quite well for me and for the other employees in my area. If I requested anything from the manager, I received it.

> When a man's ways please the LORD, he maketh even his enemies to be at peace with him.
> —PROVERBS 16:7

It is wonderful when a person looks forward to going to work. That was the way it was with the three of us. All of us were Christians, and we enjoyed Christ in each other. Work was fun again.

But to my surprise, my section was transferred to another area, into a building across the street. This move left Annie in charge of one area rather than three. Our new manager was calm and very efficient. Most of all, she was also a Christian.

It gets better. Two other Christian women were integrated into our area. All six employees were believers. We might still have a standing record as the only Christian laboratory in the history of medical laboratories.

Our roster read as follows: two Pentecostals, three Southern Baptists, and one Roman Catholic. I never heard any of us deride another's faith. We had the utmost respect for one another. It was not a hard thing because the Holy Spirit shed the love of Christ abroad in our hearts.

> By this shall all men know that ye are my disciples, if ye have love one to another.
> —JOHN 13:35

We shared together outside of the workplace. We learned the real meaning of Paul's words:

> There is neither Jew nor Greek, there is neither bond nor free, there is neither male nor female: for ye are all one in Christ Jesus.
> —GALATIANS 3:28

Each one of us knew that God was in our midst, and each of us relished His presence.

> For where two or three are gathered together in my name, there am I in the midst of them.
> —MATTHEW 18:20

> ...[F]or he hath said, I will never leave thee, nor forsake thee.
> —HEBREWS 13:5

We praised Him, praised Him, and praised Him for an ideal work situation. It was simply glorious. Once more, I thought it could not get any better. I was wrong again.

Little did I know that another move was in the plan. However, after a while, we were again transferred to the main hospital complex to another laboratory division under the supervision of yet another person.

At the time, I did not understand the reason for these moves. They did not make sense. Later I heard that our second move happened because our superiors were concerned for our safety. We had been working in a building that was somewhat isolated from the main hospital setup, and this meant that we were alone on the weekends. Additionally, all kinds of people had access to the halls and parking lots of the building. I can understand their concern.

Moving the entire laboratory was difficult. Highly technical and analytical equipment had to be transported from one area to another. There could be no down time for some tests, and this meant that some courageous technologist had to perform tests even as other equipment was being removed from around her.

After the day's results were released, the last of the equipment was moved and set up for the next day's work.

It was an arduous process, but God gave us strength and endurance. Not only were we moving, but God was moving also. Justice had to be rendered on my behalf. He was taking me from Egypt to Canaan. I had been afflicted in Egypt; Canaan was a place of blessings and restoration. I will admit that all of us hated to depart our safe haven, but we stood on the Word of God.

> And we know that all things work together for good to them that love God, to them who are the called according to his purpose.
>
> —ROMANS 8:28

> I will cry unto God most high; unto God that performeth all things for me. He shall send from heaven, and save me from the reproach of him that would swallow me up. Selah. God shall send forth his mercy and his truth.
>
> —PSALM 57:2–3

Our new work environment consisted of many non-Christians. They were nice people, but non-Christians. Some were not even churchgoers.

In a short while, we realized why the Lord had thrust us out of our comfort zone. The Lord—not the physicians—had need of us among a new people, an unsaved people. We were careful not to badger anyone; neither did we impose our beliefs upon our coworkers.

We were even more careful to let our lights shine and to maintain good works.

> Ye are the light of the world. A city that is set on an hill cannot be hid. Neither do men light a candle, and put it under a bushel, but on a candlestick; and it giveth light unto all that are in the house. Let your light so shine before men, that they may see your good works, and glorify your Father which is in heaven.
>
> —MATTHEW 5:14–16

> The people which sat in darkness saw great light; and to them which sat in the region and shadow of death light is sprung up.
>
> —MATTHEW 4:16

Our presence made a significant impact, and the move of God was awesome. Some of the personnel who had not attended church on a regular basis became regular attenders. They purchased new Bibles, sought our counsel, asked for prayer, and even came to some of our church functions.

The Lord gave me great favor with my immediate supervisor and coworkers. It was common knowledge that only 1 percent of the employees could receive an outstanding rating on evaluations. I was one of the blessed few. Praise Him!

Finally, I made it to Canaan. It was a good land, a land with brooks of water and fountains that sprang out of valleys and hills.

> A land of wheat, and barley, and vines, and fig trees, and pomegranates; a land of oil olive, and honey; a land wherein thou shalt eat bread without scarceness, thou shalt not lack any thing in it; a land whose stones are iron, and out of whose hills thou mayest dig brass.
>
> —DEUTERONOMY 8:8–9

> When thou hast eaten and art full, then thou shalt bless the LORD thy God for the good land which he hath given thee.
>
> —DEUTERONOMY 8:10

By His grace, I remember to bless Him.

> So the LORD blessed the latter end of Job more than his beginning.
>
> —JOB 42:12

Chapter 24

Tired of Sunday Work

⟍⟋⟍

OST MEDICAL-LABORATORY PERSONNEL are required to work weekends. I surmise that medical technologists—those who do the actual testing—work one out of four weekends on average. Of course, the average may vary, depending upon the setting. Weekend work was sometimes difficult, tiring, and stressful. The staff was limited, and many times the workload equaled or exceeded that of a fully staffed workday.

The area in which I was employed did a tedious form of cardiac testing. The analyses we performed supplied physicians with information that aided them in the diagnosis of heart attacks. So it made good sense that the tests were done seven days a week.

As I stated above, the weekend staff was limited. In my area, Special Chemistry, one technologist was responsible for the entire workload. On many occasions, I was that one person. Most technologists were not as adversely affected by the Sunday scheduling as I was. I taught the Sunday school class for young adults and was also the announcer during our morning worship service.

The evening broadcast service began at seven o'clock. Sometimes I left the laboratory as late as five thirty or six o'clock totally exhausted. The saints—especially the older ones—prayed for me. They were concerned about the long, tiring hours I worked on weekends.

I was aware that they were sincerely praying, but I could not conceive of not working on Sunday. After all, everyone else did, and I thought I had to also. *The nature of the job dictates that I work on the Lord's day. Heart attacks are not respecters of days, right? Apparently, I don't have a choice in the matter,* I thought. So I went along with the decision of my superiors.

God asked Abraham:

> Is any thing too hard for the Lord?
>
> —Genesis 18:14

> And the Lord said unto Moses, Is the Lord's hand waxed short?
>
> —Numbers 11:23

> Behold, I am the Lord, the God of all flesh: is there any thing too hard for me?
>
> —Jeremiah 32:27

Finally, the appointed day came, the day when I gave it to the Lord. As I left my workplace I was tired, tired, tired. Not only was I tired *from* the work, but I was also tired *of* the work.

> For verily I say unto you, That whosoever shall say unto this mountain, Be thou removed, and be thou cast into the sea; and shall not doubt in his heart, but shall believe that those things which he saith shall come to pass; he shall have whatsoever he saith.
>
> —Mark 11:23

The most powerful nine words of my lifetime may have been "Lord, I am so tired of working on Sundays." Finally, I believed, and I finally said it.

> The king's heart is in the hand of the Lord, as the rivers of water: he turneth it whithersoever he will.
>
> —Proverbs 21:1

> For my thoughts are not your thoughts, neither are your ways my ways, saith the Lord. For as the heavens are higher than the earth, so are my ways higher than your ways, and my thoughts than your thoughts.
>
> —Isaiah 55:8–9

Man's extremity is God's opportunity.

The news was announced on Thursday of the same week. The administration and the physicians had decided that we would no longer do cardiac testing on Sundays. They had concluded that tests completed in other areas were sufficient to make a prognosis and that our testing would be done on Mondays. Our results would be used as confirmatory information.

Yes, I had subjected myself to years of discomfort because I did not trust God for deliverance. I was trying to figure it out. I could not see. I couldn't believe. Not only is He able, but He is well able.

> With men this is impossible; but with God all things are possible.
>
> —MATTHEWS 19:26

Chapter 25

Guidelines for Suffering on the Job

Blessed be God, even the Father of our Lord Jesus Christ,
the Father of mercies, and the God of all comfort; Who
comforteth us in all our tribulation, that we may be able
to comfort them which are in any trouble, by the comfort wherewith we ourselves are comforted of God.

—2 CORINTHIANS 1:3–4

THE LORD HAS used my testimony to bless the body of
Christ. Many have shared that when adversity came their
way, they performed a mental replay of the story of God's
work in my life. "Now what would Evangelist Matthews do?"
they asked.

Some people call and ask me to analyze their work situations.
The enemy is Satan. No matter where he is, his tactics are the
same. He comes to steal, kill, and destroy, as John 10:10 reveals.
In the same verse, however, Jesus promised, "I am come that they
might have life, and that they might have it more abundantly."

Yes, I blundered along the way, but the grace of God was my
staying power.

If thou faint in the day of adversity, thy strength is
small.

—PROVERBS 24:10

78

There were times when I had to say, "I'm sorry, Lord; forgive me. I really shouldn't have said that. Keep love in my heart for my enemy."

> But I say unto you, Love your enemies, bless them that curse you, do good to them that hate you, and pray for them which despitefully use you, and persecute you; That ye may be the children of your Father which is in heaven: for he maketh his sun to rise on the evil and on the good, and sendeth rain on the just and on the unjust.
>
> —MATTHEW 5:44–45

A large percentage of employees, believers as well as unbelievers, have problems on their jobs. It is an absolute must for a Christian to know that he is in the will of God in every area of his life. His relationships—in his place of employment, his church home, and the school that he attends—should be ordered providentially. Salary is not the determinant in selecting a job—God is.

I cannot stress enough the importance of knowing God's will for your life, and not just knowing it, but walking therein.

> Trust in the LORD with all thine heart; and lean not unto thine own understanding.
>
> —PROVERBS 3:5

1. At the first sign of trouble, go to God in prayer and ask Him, "Lord, why is this happening to me?"

If He reveals unconfessed sin in your life, repent immediately. Look at Jonah, for example. God commissioned Jonah to go to Nineveh.

> Now the word of the LORD came unto Jonah the son of Amittai, saying, Arise, go to Nineveh, that great city, and cry against it; for their wickedness is come up before me.
>
> —JONAH 1:1–2

But Jonah rose up to flee unto Tarshish from the presence of the Lord, and went down to Joppa; and he found a ship going to Tarshish: so he paid the fare thereof, and went down into it, to go with them unto Tarshish from the presence of the Lord. But the Lord sent out a great wind into the sea, and there was a mighty tempest in the sea, so that the ship was like to be broken..

—Jonah 1:3–4

So they took up Jonah, and cast him forth into the sea: and the sea ceased from her raging.

—Jonah 1:15

Now the Lord had prepared a great fish to swallow up Jonah. And Jonah was in the belly of the fish three days and three nights.

—Jonah 1:17

They that observe lying vanities forsake their own mercy. But I will sacrifice unto thee with the voice of thanksgiving; I will pay that that I have vowed. Salvation is of the Lord. And the Lord spake unto the fish, and it vomited out Jonah upon the dry land.

—Jonah 2:8–10

When Jonah repented and came back to the place of consecration and obedience, the Lord spoke to the fish, and it vomited him out. Jonah obeyed after he was commissioned the second time. He did his duty at last.

2. If you are being tried—get ready, set, go! The fight is on. And guess what? You are the winner!

Remind yourself daily: *I am the winner!* You will have times when you do not feel victorious, but know that God "giveth us the victory through our Lord Jesus Christ" (1 Cor. 15:57).

Many are the afflictions of the righteous: but the Lord delivereth him out of them all.

—Psalm 34:19

She that hath borne seven languisheth: she hath given up the ghost; her sun is gone down while it was yet day: she hath been ashamed and confounded: and the residue of them will I deliver to the sword before their enemies, saith the LORD.

—JEREMIAH 15:9

I can hear you saying, "Lord, what is going on? I don't understand."

Beloved, think it not strange concerning the fiery trial which is to try you, as though some strange thing happened unto you.

—1 PETER 4:12

At the onset of a trial, the time of complexity, "we see through a glass, darkly" and only "know in part" (1 Cor. 13:12). I visualize God as a parent who feels very sorry for his child when the doctor gives him a shot. Although the child screams, kicks, and hollers because of the pain inflicted by the needle, a wise parent does not reject the shot. The parent knows that the pain is temporary and the medicine in the needle will perfect healing within the child's body.

We scream, kick, and holler in our trials, and the Lord feels our pain. But He knows that an injection of affliction will "perfect, stablish, strengthen, settle [us]" (1 Pet. 5:10).

Before I was afflicted I went astray: but now have I kept thy word.

—PSALM 119:67

3. Suffer as a Christian.

But let none of you suffer as a murderer, or as a thief, or as an evildoer, or as a busybody in other men's matters. Yet if any man suffer as a Christian, let him not be ashamed; but let him glorify God on this behalf.

—1 PETER 4:15–16

Do not create problems for yourself by talking to your coworkers about issues that adversely affect you in the workplace. As a rule, a wounded individual will talk to anyone who will listen. Most often, when the burdens are lifted from that person, he tends to regret the words he spoke.

> A word fitly spoken is like apples of gold in pictures of silver.
> —PROVERBS 25:11

4. Employees are commanded to answer to their employers according to biblical principles.

> Servants, be obedient to them that are [your] masters according to the flesh, with fear and trembling, in single-ness of your heart, as unto Christ; not with eyeservice, as menpleasers; but as the servants of Christ, doing the will of God from the heart; with good will doing service, as to the Lord, and not to men: knowing that whatsoever good thing any man doeth, the same shall he receive of the Lord, whether he be bond or free.
> —EPHESIANS 6:5–8

5. Spend as much time as possible with the Lord, in prayer and reading His Word. Take advantage of any break to be alone with Him.

I was blessed to work at an institution that housed several chapels. One chapel in particular was my safe haven, my ark of safety, and my city of refuge. It was where I went to regroup. I used the tools of prayer, meditation, and reading the Word of God. Even now, I can hardly walk past that chapel without stopping to look in.

Although you might not have access to a literal chapel, there is a place of solitude in each job situation. Find that place, and meet the Lord there. He will be faithful to be punctual and to make His presence known. Give yourself to constant, faithful prayer. Let God make your prayer life a life of prayer. As you go on to know God, He will reveal Satan's plans to you and will give you the weapons you need to thwart them.

6. Don't retaliate. Walk in love.

> Dearly beloved, avenge not yourselves, but rather give place unto wrath: for it is written, Vengeance is mine; I will repay, saith the Lord. Therefore if thine enemy hunger, feed him; if he thirst, give him drink: for in so doing thou shalt heap coals of fire on his head. Be not overcome of evil, but overcome evil with good.
>
> —ROMANS 12:19–21

> Say not thou, I will recompense evil; but wait on the LORD, and he shall save thee.
>
> —PROVERBS 20:22

Never say that you will do something you cannot do in faith. Pray to God for His assistance against the desire to take revenge. We must refer ourselves to God and leave it to Him—in His way and in His time—to plead our cause, maintain our right, and reckon with those who do us wrong. Wait on the Lord, attend His pleasure, acquiesce to His will.

God does not say that He will punish those who have injured us. Instead, He desires that we forgive them and pray for them. He will save us, and that is enough. He will protect us, so that our passing by one injury will not, as is commonly feared, expose us to another. No, He will recompense good to us, to balance our trouble and encourage our patience.

7. Defy bitterness.

Rebuke it and bind it. Bind bitterness, and loose the power of the Holy Spirit to move in you. For example, you can pray as follows:

> *Satan, in the name of Jesus, I bind you and the spirit of bitterness, according to Matthew 18:18, which clearly states, "Whatsoever ye shall bind on earth shall be bound in heaven." This verse further promises that "whatsoever ye shall loose on earth shall be loosed in heaven." I loose the power of the Holy Spirit in my life to restore and fill me with His power.*

Trials and tests come to make us better, not bitter.

Let all bitterness, and wrath, and anger, and clamour, and
evil speaking, be put away from you, with all malice.
—EPHESIANS 4:31

8. Remind yourself that it is a trial.

God has given Satan permission to come against us. The
enemy can do nothing without divine permission. When God
gives permission, He sets limits on Satan's powers.

Lord, why am I broke? It's a trial.
Lord, why am I being persecuted? It's a trial.
Lord, why are my children acting up? It's a trial.
Lord, why did I lose my job? It's a trial.

But he knoweth the way that I take: when he hath tried
me, I shall come forth as gold.
—JOB 23:10

Wherein ye greatly rejoice, though now for a season, if
need be, ye are in heaviness through manifold tempta-
tions: that the trial of your faith, being much more pre-
cious than of gold that perisheth, though it be tried with
fire, might be found unto praise and honour and glory at
the appearing of Jesus Christ.
—1 PETER 1:6–7

9. Praise Him, praise Him, praise Him.

Do not wait until you feel like praising the Lord. We will not
feel like it at times, especially during the early stages of trials.

But thou art holy, O thou that inhabitest the praises of
Israel.
—PSALM 22:3

Praise will bring the presence of God. Although God is everywhere present, there is a distinct manifestation of His rule, which
enters the environment of praise. Praise is the remedy for times
when we feel alone, deserted, or depressed.

The word *inhabit* (*yawshab* in Hebrew) means "to sit down, to
remain, to settle or marry." In other words, God does not merely
visit us when we praise Him. Instead, His presence abides with

us, and we partner with Him in a growing relationship. Let this truth create faith and trust and lead to deliverance from satanic harassment, torments, or bondage.

10. Ask others to pray that God will give you the strength to endure.

During the course of the trial at my job, I called prayer warriors many times and solicited their prayers. Some days I did not have the strength to pray for myself. I really did not want to pray for myself; I just wanted to go home, never to return. But the prayers of the saints encouraged me to "stand still, and see the salvation of the LORD" (Exod. 14:13).

11. Commit your situation to the Lord.

> Commit thy way unto the LORD; trust also in him; and he shall bring it to pass.
>
> —PSALM 37:5

12. Wait on the Lord. Wait for your deliverance!

> I waited patiently for the LORD; and he inclined unto me, and heard my cry. He brought me up also out of an horrible pit, out of the miry clay, and set my feet upon a rock, and established my goings. And he hath put a new song in my mouth, even praise unto our God: many shall see it, and fear, and shall trust in the LORD.
>
> —PSALM 40:1–3

> *Rest in* the LORD, and *wait patiently* for *him.*
>
> —PSALM 37:7, AUTHOR'S EMPHASIS

Notes

Chapter 18

Cover My Car With Your Blood

1. Benny Hinn, *The Blood* (Lake Mary, FL: Creation House, 1993), 20–21.
2. H.A. Maxwell Whyte, *The Power of the Blood* (New Kensington, PA: Whitaker House, 2005).
3. Hinn, 17.